# STOLEN INNOCENCE

by:
KJ GoForth

**Gotham Books**

30 N Gould St.
Ste. 20820, Sheridan, WY 82801
https://gothambooksinc.com/

Phone: 1 (307) 464-7800

© 2023 *KJ GoForth*. All rights reserved.

No part of this book may be reproduced, stored in a retrieval system, or transmitted by any means without the written permission of the author.

Published by Gotham Books (October 24, 2023)

ISBN: 979-8-88775-698-1 (H)
ISBN: 979-8-88775-696-7 (P)
ISBN: 979-8-88775-697-4 (E)

Because of the dynamic nature of the Internet, any web addresses or links contained in this book may have changed since publication and may no longer be valid.

The views expressed in this work are solely those of the author and do not necessarily reflect the views of the publisher, and the publisher hereby disclaims any responsibility for them.

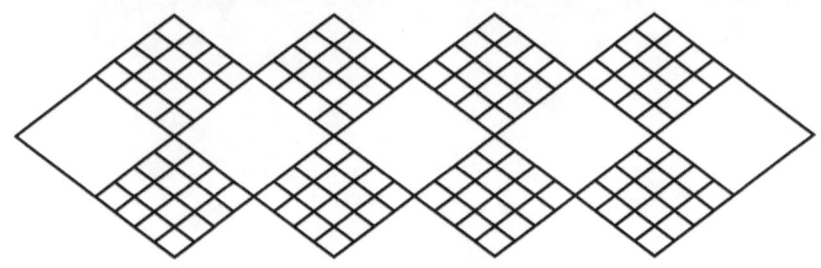

More than enough no time to waste
But not driven out of haste

Another lifetime on the cosmic wheel
With a message to reveal

Trust in self detach without
Don't let control seize doubt

What was learnt what's been learned
What in life must be earned

Birdbath fountains grassy fields
Love and kindness pays in yields

Ability to laugh no fear to cry
No more box I won't be shy

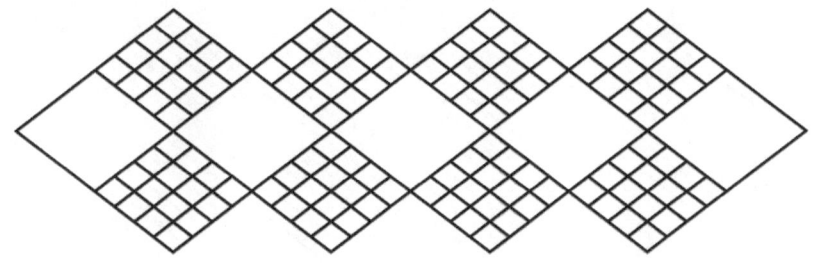

Depleted dignity reputations shot
What is owned what is not

Disturbed destructive tearing down
What the soul now has found

No regrets guilt not real
Fear and shame have no zeal

Only lessons lived to learn
Etched within the place I burn

With compassion open sights
Made it through the dark soul nights

Glad to be alive and well
Have outgrown another shell

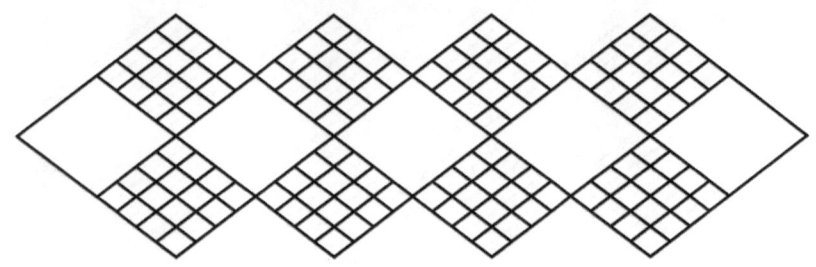

Extraordinary turn of events
About face to feel intense

Path averted dead end street
With broken glass upon my feet

Almost tricked back to pain
Stuck with wisdom to maintain

Not gonna waste what's been gained
On an avenue with restrain

Set free to fly wingspan broad
Firearm and fishing rod

Weary warrior made a new
Who's up next maybe you

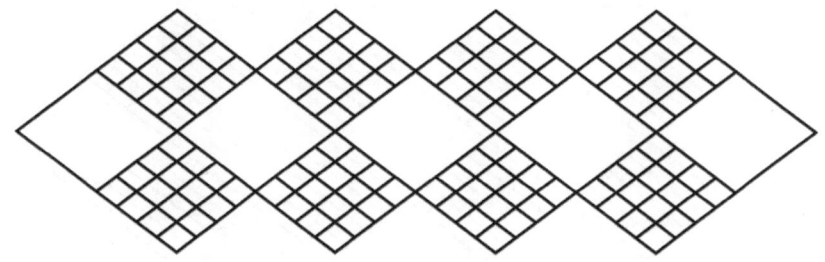

*Forever and after human disaster*

*Selling out from within*
*resetting issues that have been*

*Secret in motion selecting few*
*Circular sensation then became two*

*Adams orbs DNA*
*Elusive answers with big pay*

*Deniers dancing on false facts*
*Looking in between the cracks*

*Clouded judgment reins supreme*
*As the children cry and scream*

*Dirty deeds done dirt cheap*
*Upon our free will they do creep*

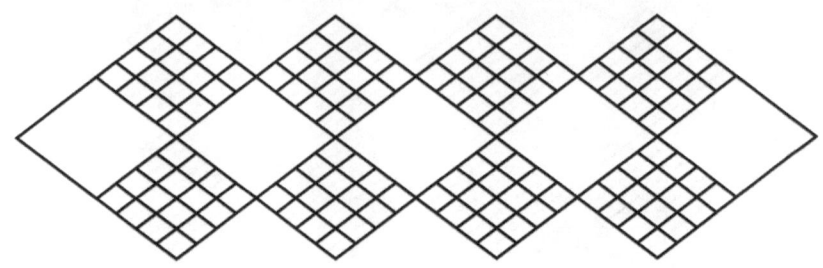

Altered reality blurring the line
Of what is and what is fine

Ripe conditions holding out hope
Won't give in I just say nope

Guarded gate castle walls
Clouds are growing as rain falls

Wealth of knowledge wisdoms child
In the dessert of the wild

Eclipsing benchmarks previous plan
Rules and labels not a fan

Safety in numbers cant see clear
Rose colored glasses living in fear

Inside and out lifes but a dream
Forward in motion with my team

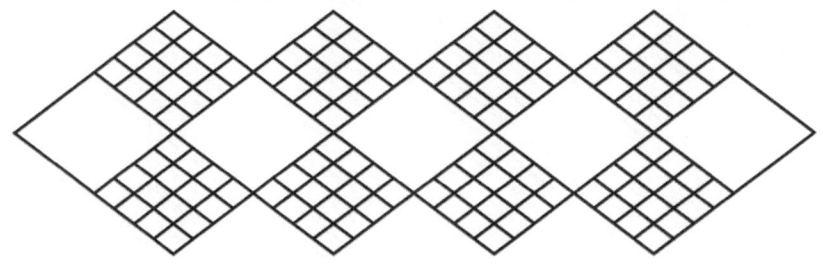

Congregation of the dead
Spiritually depleted by way of the head

Heads a bow knees a kneel
Funny headwear what's the deal

Traditions passed down with their flaws
Generations lost to a nefarious cause

Salvation soldier soldier up
Here comes a storm to wash away your cup

Lunatics liars bent on greed
Without true vision of a dying seed

Godspeed prayer to bring it home
Recreate a space unknown

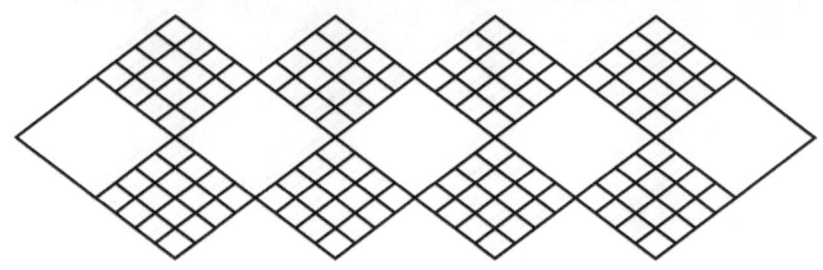

*Overcoming what had become*
*Whatever influences that made me dumb*

*Held back for what environment stale*
*Carrying sand in a full pail*

*Bricks on my back weight of the world*
*Back on my path words have been hurled*

*Gratitude grown thankful thought*
*Burrowing under each given plot*

*Resources at hand reached from the depth*
*All of the wisdom that this body has kept*

*Imagery vessels mountains moved*
*No one or nothing can ruin this groove*

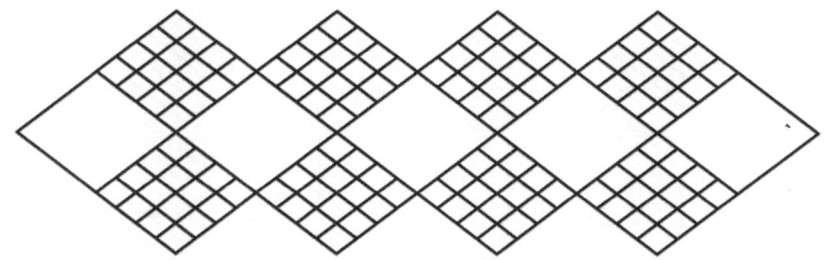

Been in love since the start
You the one that holds this heart

Forever and always every time
Brought together by divine

Lessons learned cleared to fly
Don't let this love pass you by

Fixed and solid golden globe
With what it takes to carry the load

Precious petals of the whole
How could I ever let you go

Compassion carried throughout lifetimes
Destined for love and rhythmic chimes

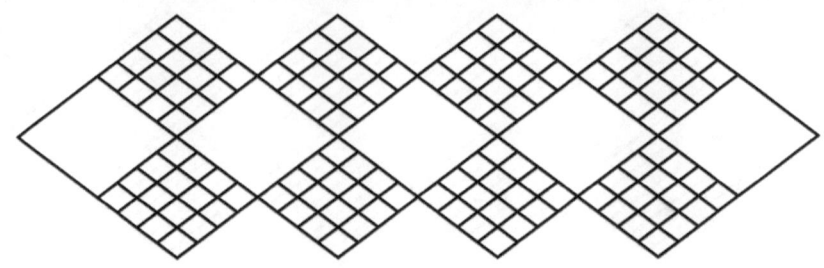

Bit and bitten by a bug
Love is a mighty powerful drug

Heart body mind and soul
Altogether on a roll

Memories slipping in the now
Evolving past the why and how

Pressing forward without expect
Enjoying what I can respect

Programs loaded redesigned
Inner kingdom brightly shined

Locked away with access
What we do each possess

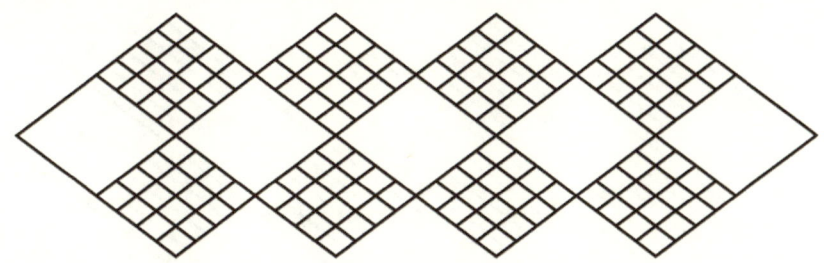

*Matter of fact circumstance*
*Of the thoughts from our pants*

*Sex seduction pleasure filled*
*Giving back what is thrilled*

*Celebrating sex calling it love*
*Nothing more than a place to shove*

*Place to waste another nut*
*Blindly firing with eyes shut*

*Love and sex not the same*
*Have only self to lay blame*

*Souls divides fractured light*
*For the whole we must fight*

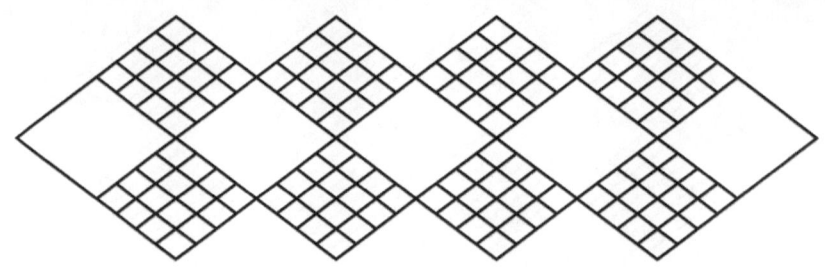

*Step up sweety look around*
*See in life what can be found*

*Be present in every moment*
*The wheel of life is truly woven*

*Stay open to some change*
*Let your heart outweigh your brains*

*Love life all you can*
*Don't let control destroy your plan*

*Authority figures come and go*
*They will try and steal your glow*

*Pour in slow pour out slow*
*Enjoy each step enjoy each show*

*Fight your own battles leave theirs to them*
*You are a warrior grow your own stem*

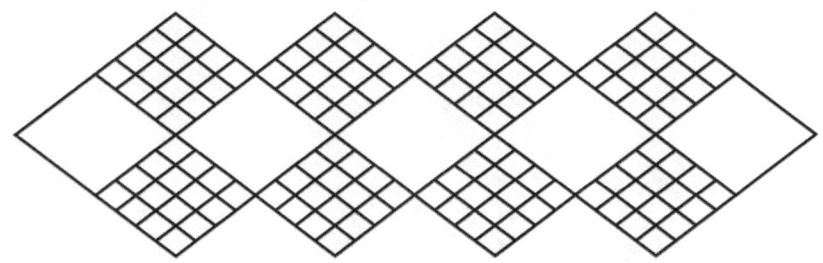

*Moving past what once was
Puberty and peach fuzz*

*Remembering the child strong and brave
That will be with me til my grave*

*Back and forth mixing moods
In a grove that exudes*

*Carefree kindness instinctual grace
With a rhythm and a pace*

*Hard to explain what could be
A life of love and merry glee*

*Abundance outflow reaping glow
Ready for some next show*

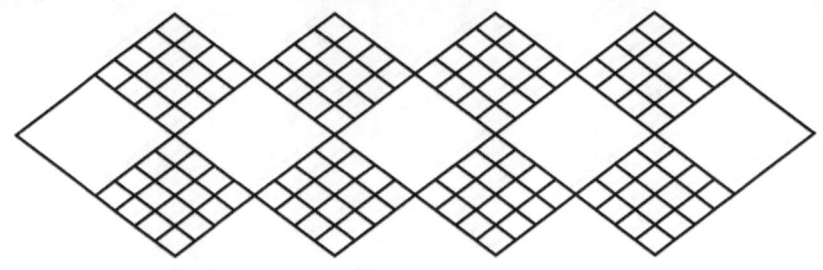

Inch given mile taken
Leaving the inch broke and shaken

Wasn't what the tears we cried
Wasn't what we hide inside

Wasn't meant wasn't true
Wasn't me wasn't you

Puzzle pieces couldn't be found
So we part on common ground

No resentments no regret
In a future that we set

In the moment in the now
Wellness outflow is the how

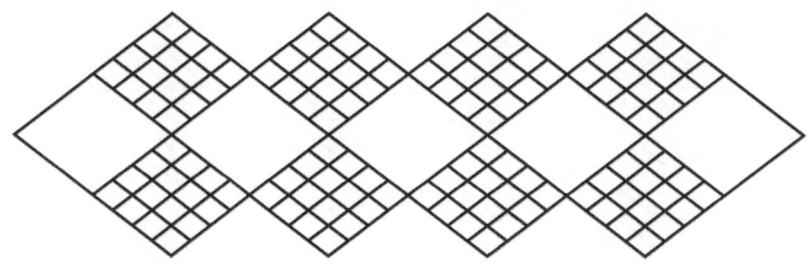

Depths of despair nowhere to go
Except for up don't cha know

Healing heartache bridging the gap
Not paying attention to any crap

Toxic talk clicks removed
Finding a new path with a new grove

Reconnected strength been found
Walking with pride on hallowed ground

No lunatic lingo can penetrate
Too intense to be berate

Loud rage silenced shock and awe
Fluidly moving now untouchable law

Mine and your love to prevail
In our own ship as we set sail

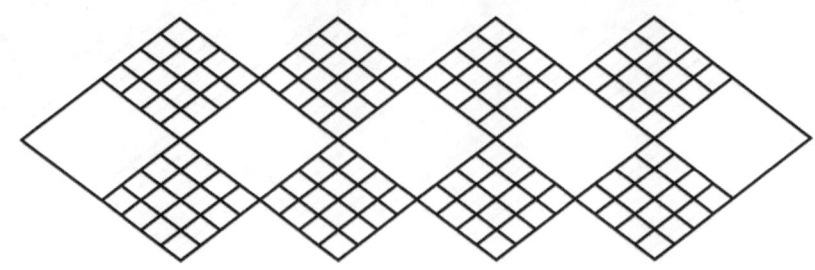

Account on hold pass the buck
What will it take to become unstuck

Pouring emotions out on this page
covering up why there is rage

Letter by letter word by word
Trying to remember what was heard

Lack of forgiveness followed by greed
Entitlement postured while the poor plead

Top of the heep as the pile grows
When will this end nobody knows

Divided by envy jealousy swirls
Winners are losers boys and girls

Dead ringer love as the heart shines
Was always the answer for all of mankind

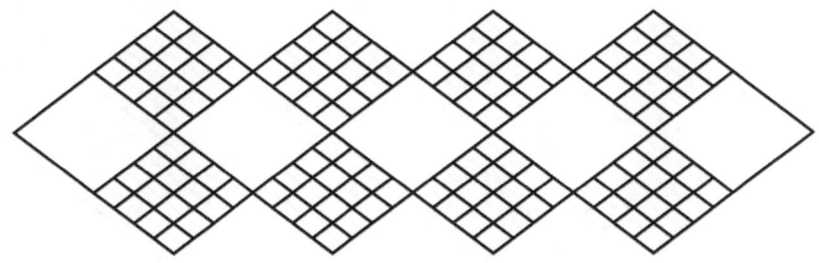

Weathering each and every storm
Getting through in fine form

Highlighting compassion free to choose
Deliverance of some news

Taught to tease strength to stand
Guided by just one hand

Trials testing every strand
Staying in tune with the cosmic band

Broad horizons setting sight
Seeing a future that will be bright

Incoming wave erasing the line
Hand and hand with the divine

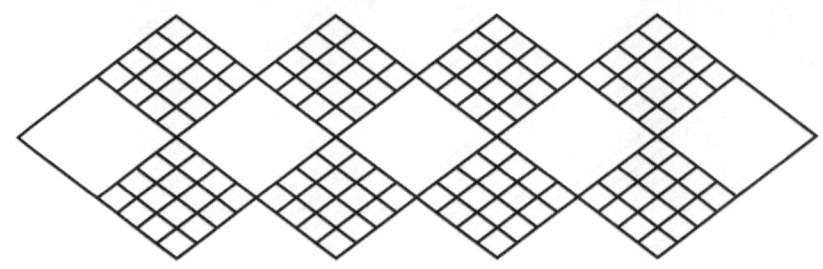

*The matrix has you your not free*
*Asking authority to take a pee*

*Projecting conformity in all forms*
*Under threat of the bull horns*

*Pastures poisoned polluted minds*
*Covering up what makes us shine*

*Barricades hurdles rings of fire*
*Keeping us from over desire*

*Beauty within creations smile*
*Worth the effort of the extra mile*

*Don't give up stay with me*
*Expand your vision of what's to be*

*You got this child just stay strong*
*Your father loves you and you do belong*

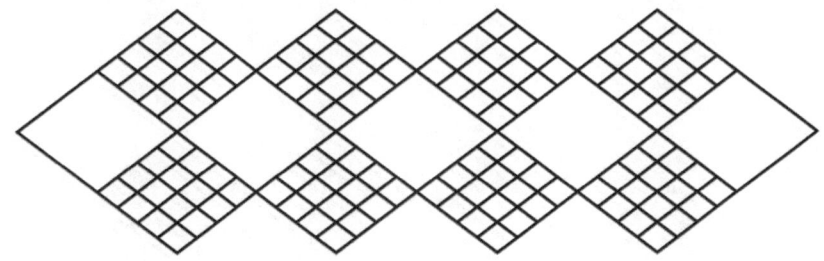

Out of love and the grip of hope
Here to throw you the life ring rope

It's my pleasure why I've come
Can't go back to what was numb

Can't imagine the gaping hole
That would be without your soul

Please hear these words beneath my breath
Start a new alive and fresh

Freedom focused your path to walk
You have always been my rock

All desires are in your house
Except that pesky thieving mouse

Keep that chip just switch shoulders
And keep writing to fill those folders

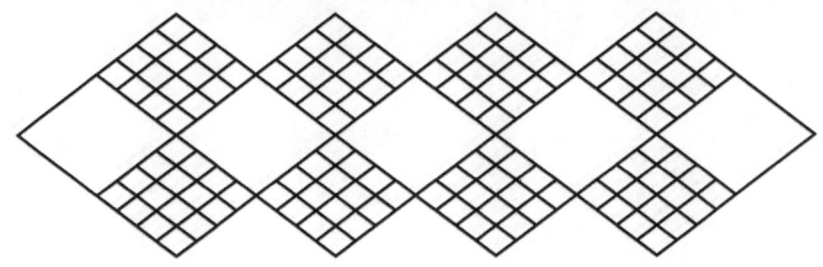

*Seekers of wisdom calling our name*
*Those of us who don't lay blame*

*Our chance to shine our chance to glow*
*Live and let live in the flow*

*Agree to disagree and move on*
*Others opinions make us pawns*

*Not our purpose to fit in*
*It's our truth that heals our kin*

*Tricks and traps will only fail*
*We must look beyond betrayal*

*Things that matter broken down*
*On our hearts we wear our crown*

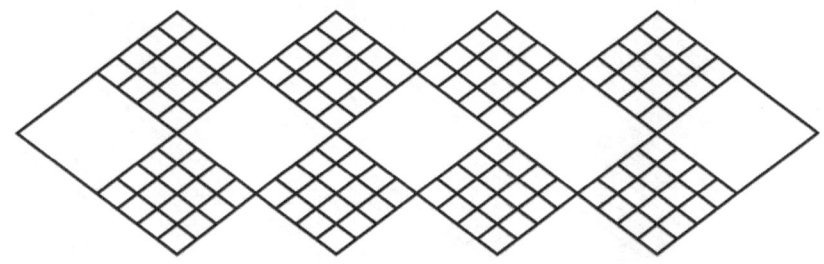

Moved by love to grow the soul
To put back what was in the hole

Sleepless nights buckets of tears
Skies are clearing without fears

Put it out there and got returned
Feeling the sensation as it burns

Gotta get through this can't be scorned
Finding the purpose as to why I was borned

Patterned behavior set aside
Not afraid of what I hide

Spiritual nature human flesh
Focused inward to become fresh

Lol me and mine
It's my turn to grow and shine

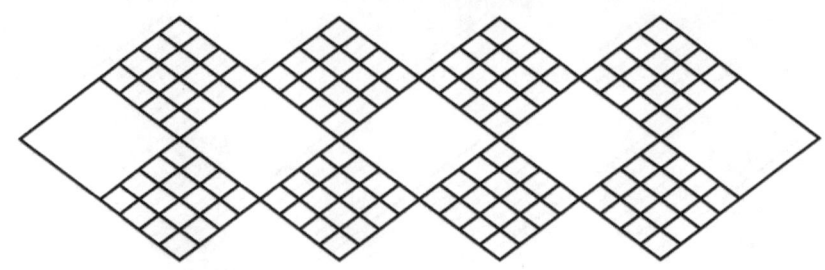

Petty disputes backing on greed
Enslaving the riches controlling seed

Histories mysteries held to be hold
Dirty secrets that have been told

Click bait calamity eating away
The further we come the more we stray

Destiny's daughter sacred womb
Here comes the hammer with a loud boom

Prisoners pictured dirty and cold
Into slavery we are sold

Fill an enigma no questions asked
History repeating blast from the past

Match has been struck pile been prepped
What we tolerate and what we accept

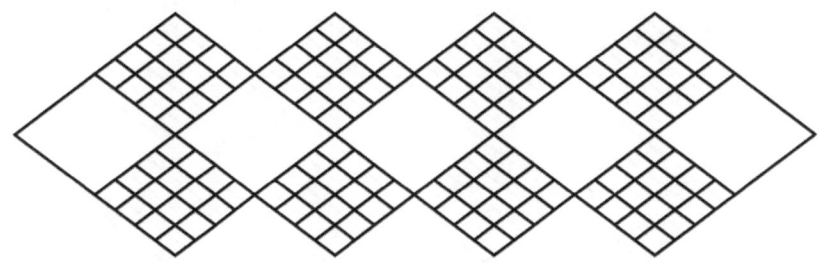

Where there is smoke there is fire
Like the anger of the liar liar

Get called out get stepped on
Squeezing the strainer before the dawn

Cleared for take off ready to launch
Smelling out what is stanch

Poisoned punch black and blue
Manipulation of me and you

Heavy headache blaming blame
No respect for what's not same

Training wheel babies cup held high
You won't be missed bye- bye- bye

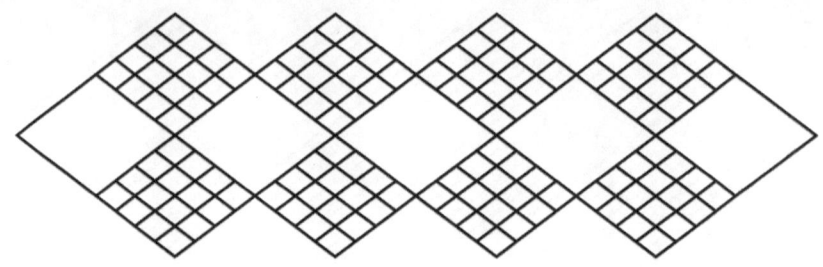

Four legs walking bushy tail
One slug moving that leaves a trail

Monkeys swinging branch to branch
Buffalo free roaming on the ranch

Butterflies flutter to and fro
Ladybug munching on mistletoe

Bumblebees buzzing all around
Groundhogs building a brand new town

Komodo dragon 3 toed sloth
Mythical creatures in the land of the lost

Astrals awning purposely placed
For our enjoyment so slow down your pace

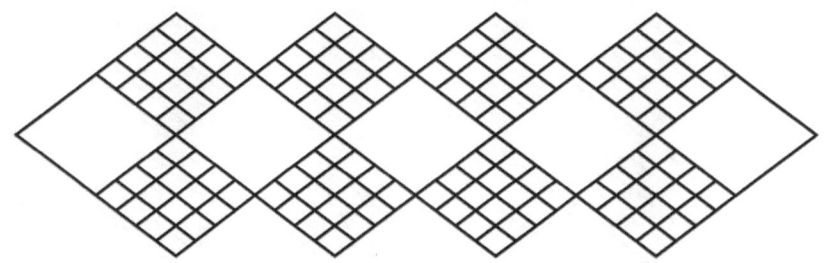

Indiscriminate targets on our backs
As we let love lay down tracks

Goals and visions carried tight
Holding them close as we fight

Squeezed to conform pressure pushed
To join some cause from someones toosh

Here to transmute what leaders lack
Through our kindness we give back

A lost tradition which will prevail
Or through the hearts will be the nail

Find the pages with what I wipe
Don't believe the false and hype

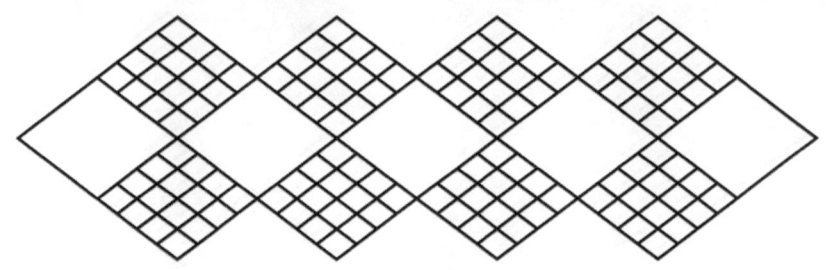

*Labels designed to separate*
*Keeping us from our fate*

*Ebb and flow time and again*
*Holding back what has been*

*Proving grounds of remembrance*
*Past and present quite intense*

*Searching the depths to what it means*
*To be human spiritual beings*

*Golden heart with white glow*
*Sharing everything I know*

*Kaleidoscope on windswept plains*
*Here to take away all our pains*

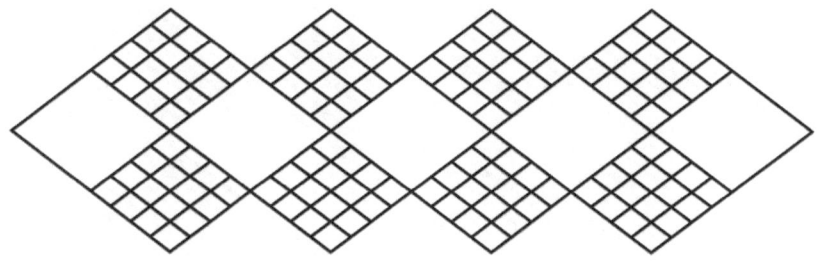

How could something so wrong seem so right
For what's in my heart I always fight

Freed from the anguish property none
Opinions on blast manipulation done

Transcending celestial compass on North
Honesty building a brand new course

Get up to go got up and gone
Reimagining a brand new dawn

Calmly courageous bravery to see
The dark and light in you and me

Pushed to the brink standing still
Hand not caught in the till

Fought to forgive free to love
Giving birth to a pure white dove

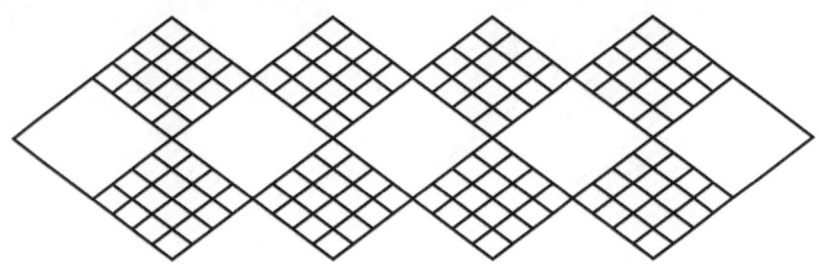

Deliberate intentional distractions guise
Mouthpiece puppets telling lies

Rebellious rebels ready for rouse
Put a cork in what conformity spews

Plug intention dismiss sick minds
Don't fall victim to their lines

Excrement coated in false hope
Like the white robe on the pope

Brutal butchery blasphemes crude
Oh you think that is rude

Check your history feel my pain
Religious dogma is quite insane

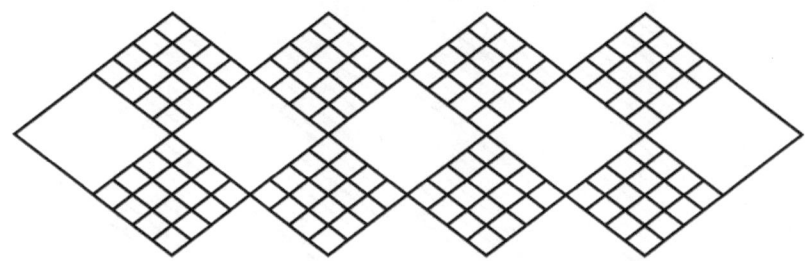

*Suddenly sad the tears I cry*
*Intuition telling me why*

*Abuse in the name of authorities guilt*
*In the houses that slave money built*

*Ruptured bloodline defective dime*
*Led by leaders who are slime*

*Brainwashed masses holy veil*
*Like to tell me i'm going to hell*

*Been there done that got my stamp*
*But now free with green light to tamp*

*Out the falsely reported words*
*Clipping the wings of us birds*

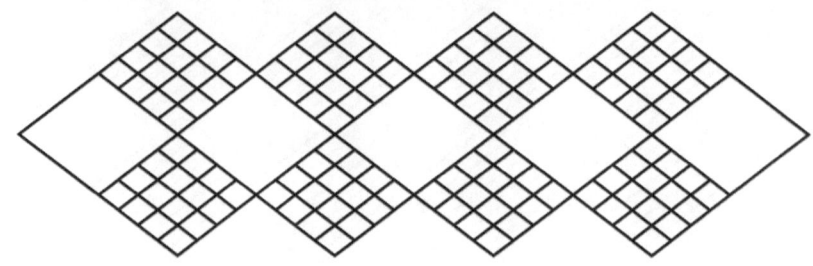

Powerful whole balanced with strength
Higher self growing in rank

Soul loss death shattering shock
Clearing out the spiritual block

Creation creator in the now
Built to pull a massive plow

Weight of the world here and gone
Ready to give what once was sawn

Loss of self shedding skin
Wanting freedom deep within

Gifted skilled wise and loud
Fitting in with the crowd

Waters parted nature's laws
Forward motion without a pause

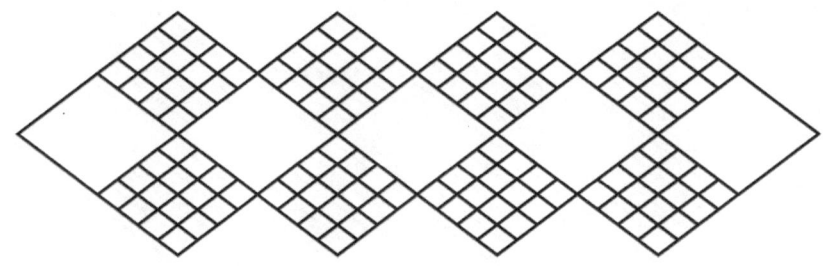

Easy to take hard to tame
Always ending up with the blame

Belonging to nowhere and nothing at the same time
Figuring life's like a rhyme

Balancing space in between
Soaking up love like a fiend

Giving back what's been given
Still feeling stuck but still believin

Maybe more trust will polish the egg
Not my style to kneel and beg

Locked in a battle dark and light
Want what I want to end this fight

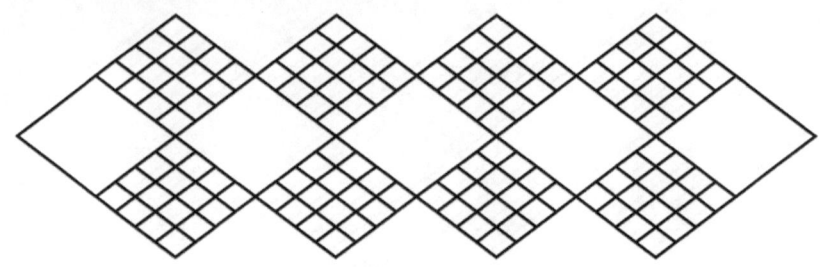

*Led to lead back to the heart*
*To try and find the missing part*

*Time after time false trials failed*
*And the heart pays as its impaled*

*Intense at the start fluttering flat*
*Slamming the door my head goes splat*

*Imagining pictures peaceful and calm*
*Then out of nowhere dropping a bomb*

*Back to my corner throw in the towel*
*Another relation that was too shallow*

*Sixty-six and rolling along*
*Doing my part to sing this hearts song*

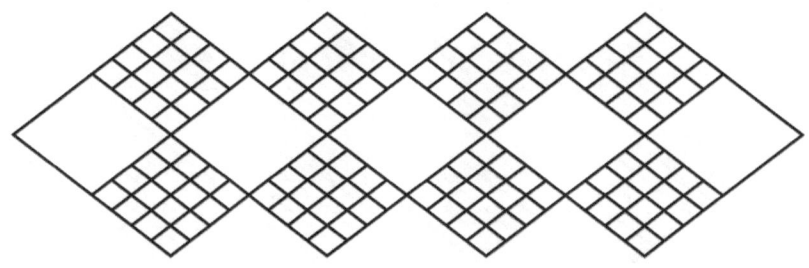

You and me back to back
Playing each card of each stack

Bonnie and Clyde Tarzan and Jane
Here to heal a world in pain

Living it up living in
A place gone mad over projected sin

Sensing a power that dwells inside
One that makes for a mighty fun ride

Astral beginnings astral ends
Joking around in the presence of friends

Hybrid heart beat DNA mix
Holding the light we get our fix

In the company of love and grace
As the tears run down our face

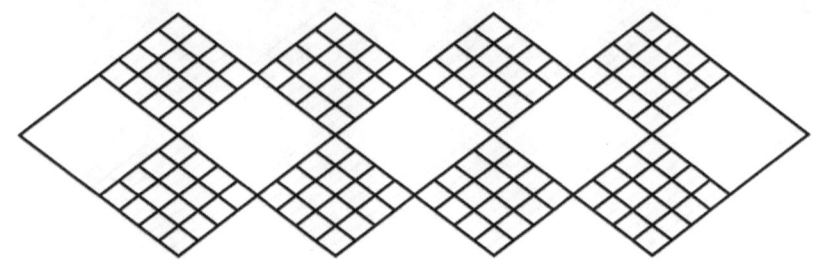

*Breaking up breaking free
Being who I want to be*

*Inventor taken bags are packed
Never never going back*

*Heart surrendered to divine
Gotta find a way to shine*

*Plastic purpose replaced with stone
For a future that's unknown*

*Glad to serve sad to say
Through our emotions we must pay*

*Worth the ride clearing crude
Out the quicksand and foul mood*

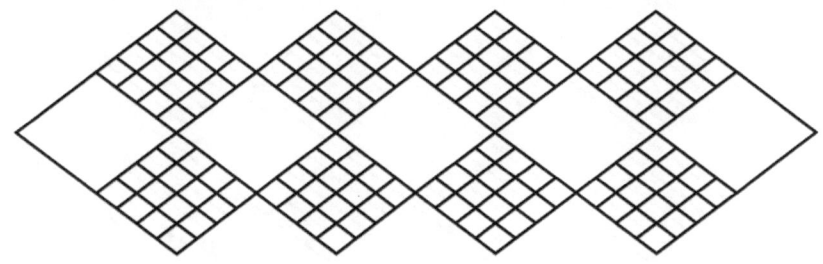

Obligations entrenched holding us back
Worn out seat with a large crack

Got my own seat made it myself
At the table I sit we all have good health

Invite only the strong and brave
Each of us fortunate to not be in a grave

Lessons been learnt baggage expunged
The weight off our backs feeling like tons

Twisting and turning navigating through
An ugly past that was stuck on with glue

Empty departing on what seems real
Anticipation of what will be revealed

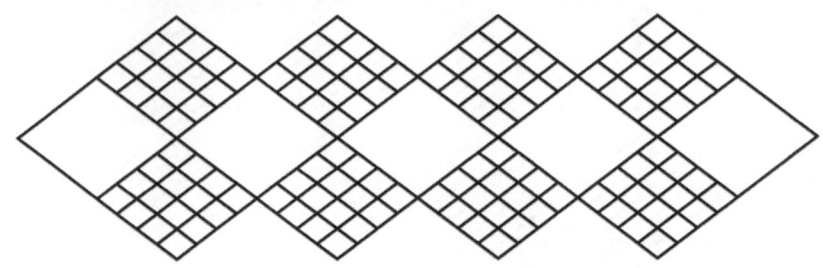

Imbued and guided spiritual rise
Control surrendered riding the highs

Good sensations coupled with love
Cosmic connection to the only dove

Created for love courted by words
Dangerous headspace frazzled nerves

Tied to trama burdensome
Rationalism confusing and numb

Patronizing gaslite camp
Aligning factions both a tramp

Pick your poison run your mouth
Globalists coming from the south

Infringing power not our friend
Ancestral wisdom will be its end

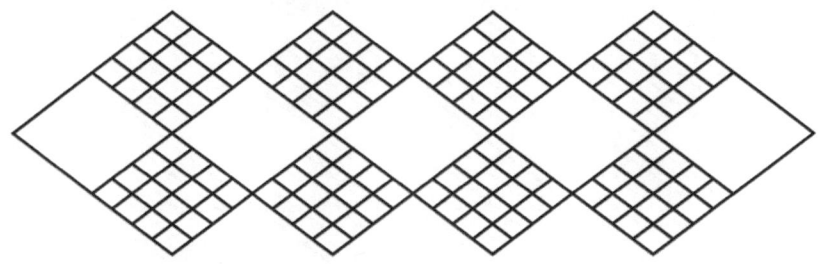

*Inspired to nurture what's inside*
*Guarded enough but not to hide*

*Freely flowing not controlled*
*Won't be bought can't be sold*

*Passing on passing through*
*What is carried in me and you*

*The brightest light a flaming torch*
*Close enough to feel its scorch*

*Collective memories passed beyond*
*Antenna tuned made of bronze*

*Sought for truth freedoms bell*
*Lifted from a life of hell*

*Laying stones brand new path*
*Free from the anger and its rath*

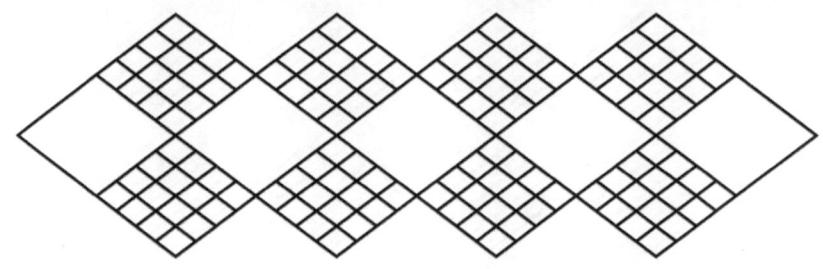

Creating love thin airs theme
Carefully aligning with the right team

Sovereign soul family independent and kind
With discernment for the blind

Limiting beliefs credited paths
Depleting life force from its crafts

Visions grown to new heights
Soulful steady to brighten dark nights

Holistic harmony part of one
Never forgetting to have fun

Being brave envelope pushed
Sitting calmly on this tush

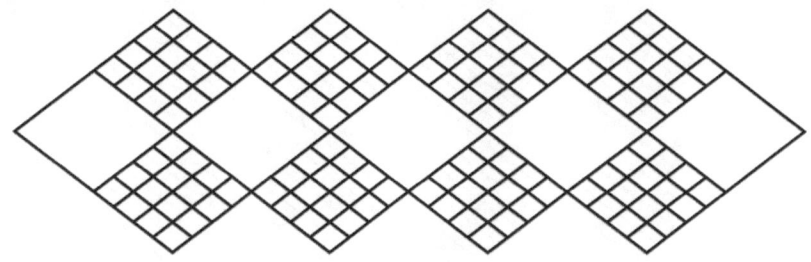

Arms extended open heart
Healing every broken part

Fragmented body wandering thoughts
Forgetting what I done gots

Pleasing sensations riddled ride
Hurting my heart and all I hide

Who what why blocking groth
Free to redefine my own oath

Love to laugh live to smile
Digging deep to run this mile

Pledged to greatness reaching high
With these wings I shall fly

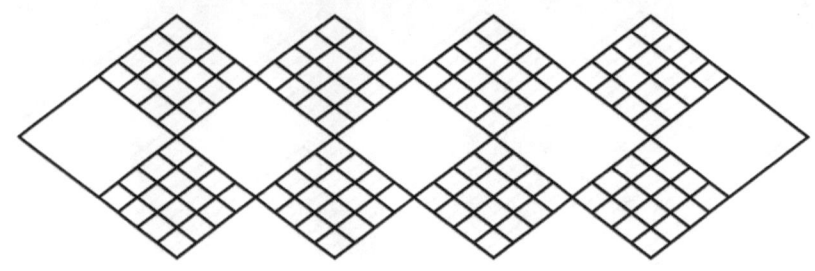

Terrorists preaching from their books
Paralyzing freedom formed by crooks

Of creation with free will
Seeing past the prophecy pill

Validation enabled codependence passed
Seeking wisdom that will last

Over boiled stew turned to mush
Humanity needing quite the push

Independent collective skilled to rise
We will be the big surprise

Left to lead in what's forgot
We won't need no vaccine shot

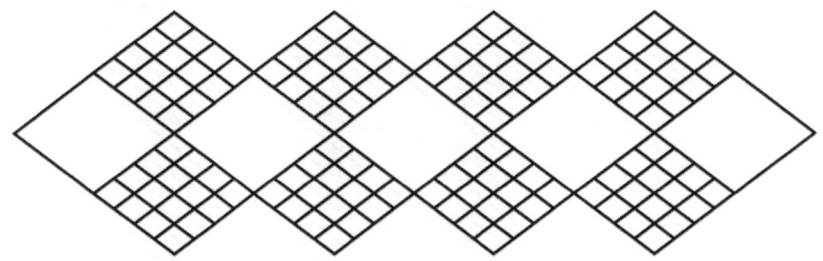

What stands out this world hates
Preventing me from my own gates

Altered opinions that don't align
Keeping me from my shine

Heavy ego rational mind
Blinded by their own kind

Gossip gurus rumors loud
I don't fit in with that crowd

Cut by anger bleeding out
From this heart booms a loud shout

Tired of tears tired of lies
Will move on in love despise

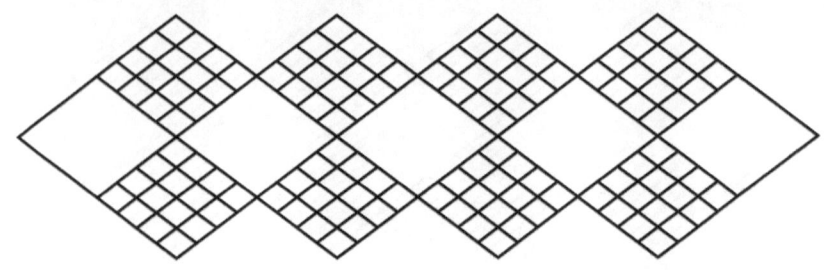

Hidden pearl inside surrounded by dark
Retreating in fear to what is stark

Bursted bubble can't go back
Holding out hope lifes not so wack

Controlling person projecting no
Gotta break free gotta let go

Body can't take it minds gone black
Anxiety fills up heart has a tack

What kind of world does this to child
What's going on influence not mild

Frivolous flaws inherited traits
Stuck in yesteryear while heaven awaits

Got my gifts got my sight
I will be strong and win this fight

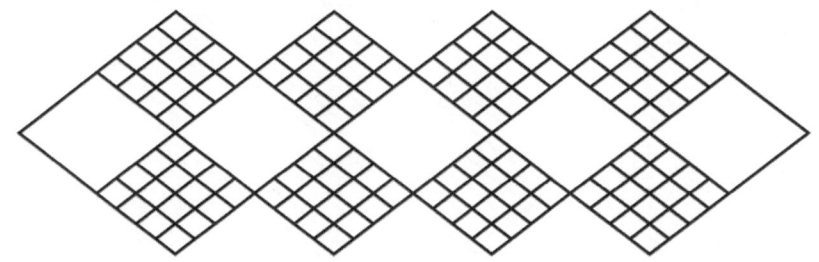

Your chance to shine all about you
Life's big lessons give you that clue

Windows with shadows broken pains
Causing a split energy drains

Fault and blame looking past
Forward to a life on blast

Arguing controls avoiding trolls
On the lookout for whole souls

Rapures rendition torn ambition
Got a mission love my fishin

Sit back sweetie enjoy the show
Feel the love and get in flow

Q-ball in hand one last shot
Give it all that you got

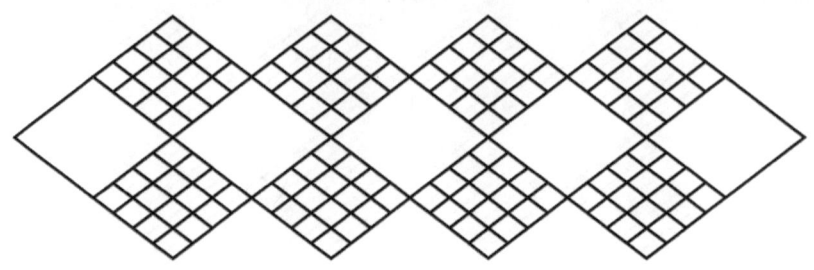

Light on the stairway kept it lit
In the cellar is where I sit

From this prospective no one knows
What is meant to let love flow

Isolation from anything kind
Teeth worn down as they grind

Barely breathing skin and bones
Facing a death from the stones

Public spectacle to right a wrong
Falsely judged by the strong

Hard to forgive betrayals mob
So I here I sit and just sob

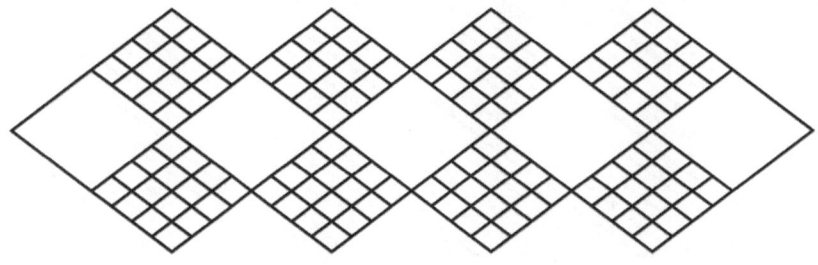

Seat of religion used to suppress
Unethical behavior in a fancy dress

Interrogation enemy exposed
Black mailers blackmailing the rows of crows

Eavesdropping proposal to rat one out
Backfire brewing to end this drought

Catch 22 impartial crusade
Emotionally trapped money paid

Co dependant to validate
Egotistical to penetrate

Indoctrination from this birth
Preying cult mind not of earth

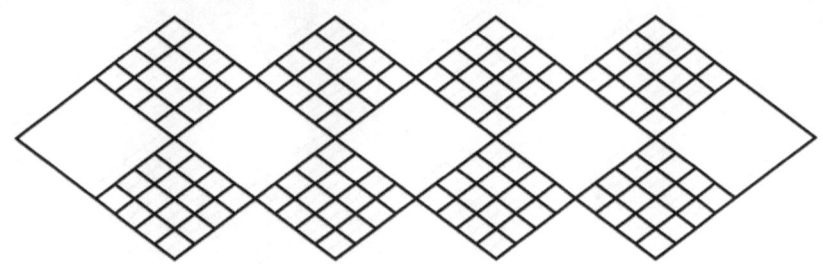

Heart space found by cupid's arrow
Penetrating my bones and its marrow

Beauty and love to what is given
Resetting again a new life for liven

In between freedoms space
Enjoying each smile on many a face

A jewel a gem a kind loving heart
Brought by the universe to be apart

Open and honest loyal and light
Bonded connection a friendship quite tight

Plate of deliverance after the pain
Healing the virtues of what was insane

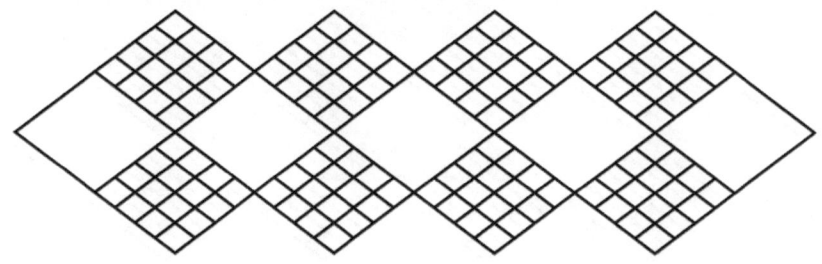

Heart of an angel on my mind
Maybe now I've found my kind

Incandescent inner glow
On the outside quite the show

Intriguing eyes soul so deep
Wondering what secrets does she keep

Profound presence lifting mood
Speechless quiet can't conclude

What was meant what will be
Free to choose wait and see

Lifetime waiting to feel secure
In this energy that's so pure

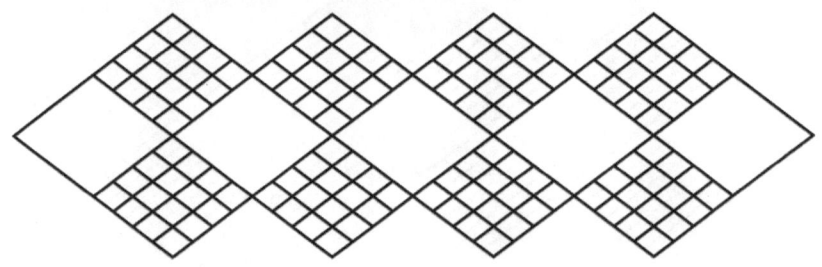

Through the long cold winters night
Your warm body fuels my light

Divine in nature pure like snow
I could never let you go

Hand in hand we walk as one
Our time together is always fun

Light and lifted ascension bound
With the gifts we have found

Awkward essence infused by love
Offer given from above

Soul path open hearts entwined
After a life where we were blind

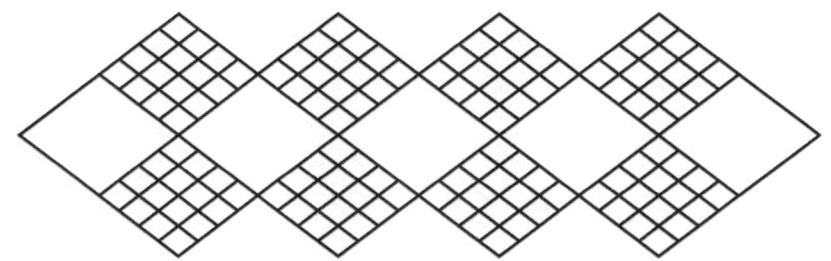

Divinities dagger hearts a flood
When we clear out all the crud

Light and happy joyous days
Lifted from realities haze

Sons and daughters children free
Playing singing sounds of glee

Caskets coffins won't exist
In the loving arms of bliss

Sharing caring loving words
No fear based thinking of the turds

Intent on purpose creative gifts
All we need within our grips

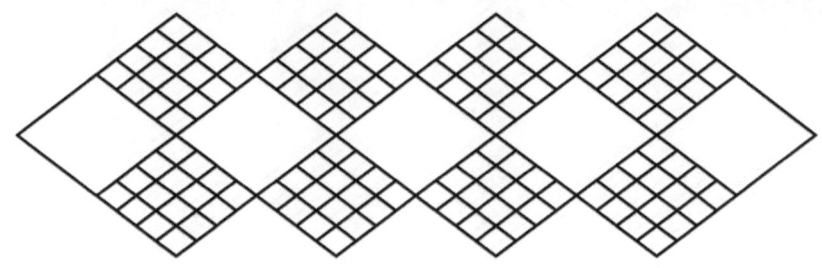

When the dark skies switch to bright
It makes us feel happy and light

Credit given creations gift
Giving us a needed lift

Light source held sacred heart
So amazing to be a part

Centuries of patience to become
What was not devised by scum

Egocentric powers hook
Believing what is in their book

Cosmic collision to raise our vibe
Exposing what we keep inside

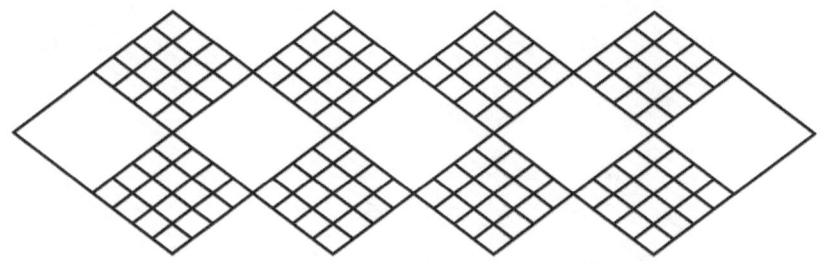

I am but my hollow self
Nothing gets in nothing gets out

Scoured and whipped clean polished pristine
On a path that no one has seen

Why me why now what's going on
One bird one feather in this new dawn

Clarity ringing projections blocked
Inner sanctum has been rocked

Spiritually awake soul rebirthed
Free to move about this earth

Loud with laughter serenading sounds
Giving the finger to false clowns

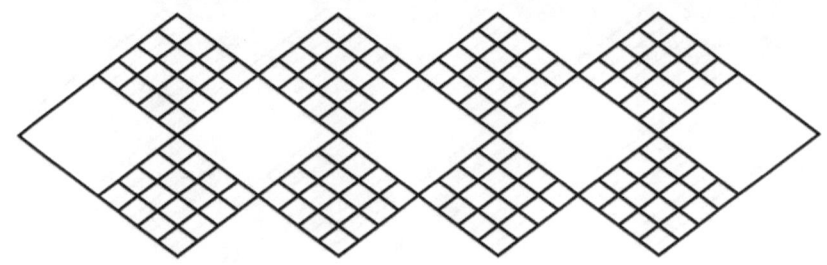

Under the shadows that I hold
Is a story that must be told

Little by little letting go
Finding the courage to heal my soul

Pain keeps washing through my being
I only care about one thing

In time I know what feels right
I can make it through this fight

A freedom promised a chance to grow
In my child like loving flow

Holding out hope change is hard
Need a new deck on last card

I can do this I am strong
I will find where I belong

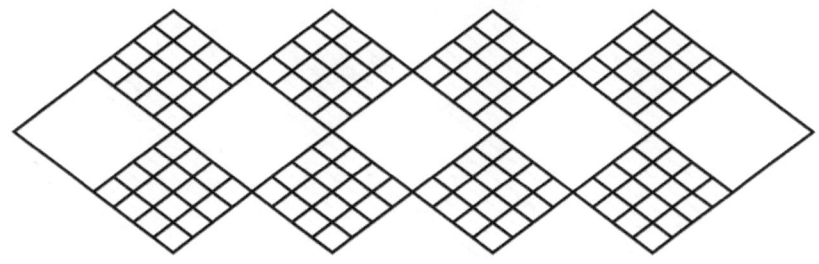

Hornets nest of the hive
Angry energy in low vibe

Defense of threat what does not fit in
Waring freelance once again

Follow the money divisive tip
Power on its head game trip

Playing both sides to ensure control
While our innocence pays the toll

Laws enforcing powers trick
Cutting the balls off every dick

East of Eden with sharp blade
Guilt complex for getting laid

Hillicostic stripped of pride
Not gonna keep this shit inside

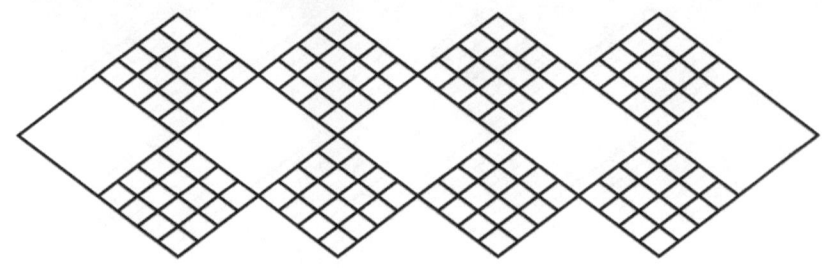

Freshly formed precedent
Whipping clear the day of lent

Egocentric father may I
Pins and needles in each eye

Permission granted authority hung
Underneath its pile of dung

Just pointing out what precists
Spiritual poverty still exists

Acquiescing for some prize
As corruption is on the rise

Brazen projection of guilt and sin
As the war chest fills again

Profiteers pray for wealth
As they sicken all our health

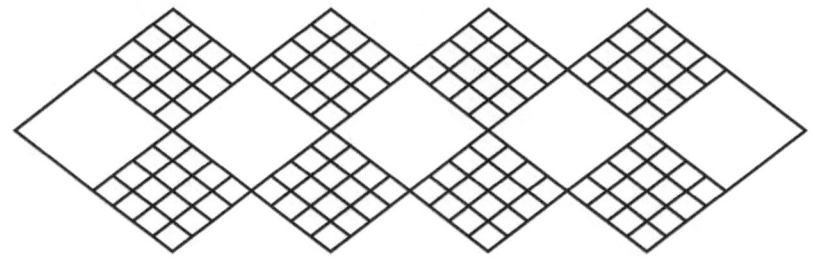

Positively made for one
Living life out of fun

Serious seduction hearts a glow
After letting all pain go

Cultivating truths adorned
Stay clear of any thorns

Brought to one knee and then two
A deep connection I can see through

Intuition high alert
As I chase another skirt

Over powered by small head
Remembering what the other head said

Life is short cautions wind
Can't hold back and won't pretend

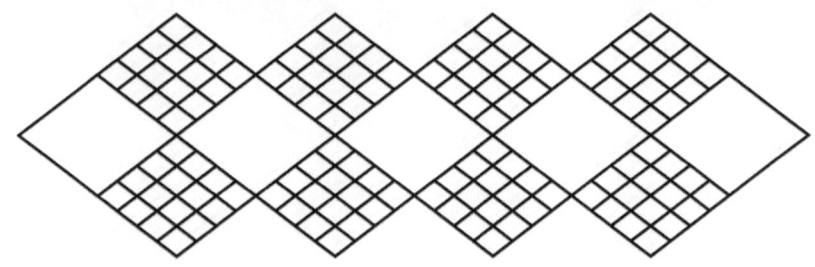

Lure of money and its stench
Carrot held out by the wench

Get on board or get left out
In a men made manipulated drought

Burning bribes pocket deep
While our patience reach a steep

Ready to boil scorching the pot
History repeats or maybe not

Collective courage aimed at peace
Is what's needed to tame each beast

Throwing what's money at more war
Only supports the dirty whore

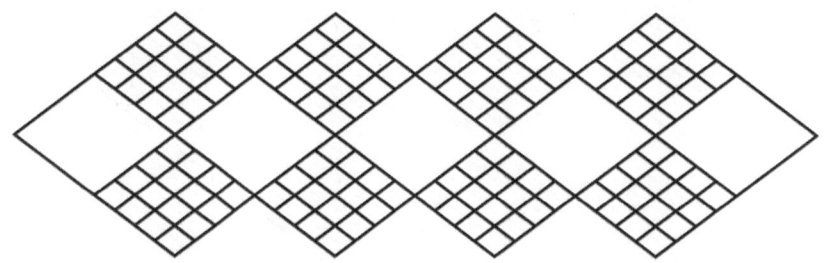

Internal torture limbs chopped off
Rope still hanging from the loft

Broken heart syndrome as it was
Tuned to love feeling the buzz

Out of body silhouettes seen
Back to where it had been

Got it wrong easy way out
Voices too loud causing doubt

Attitude altered didn't give a damn
Couldn't find answers only found spam

Black to bright blink of an eye
No more servings of American pie

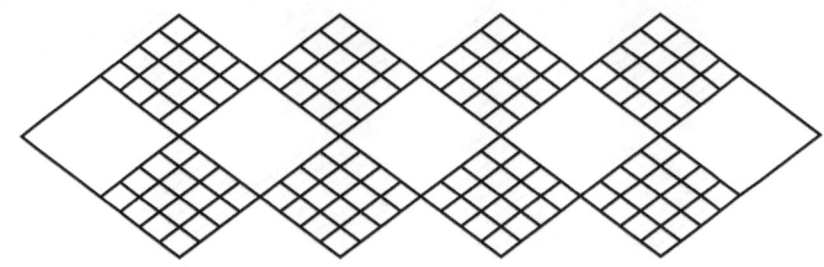

To the detriment of the self
Putting it out there like a worker elf

Karma correcting a life of deeds
At my core a soul that pleads

Fulfilling harmonic conscience cleared
In a way that I was reared

Redirected redefined
What is meant to be blind

Echoing soul to be near
The light I hold I use to fear

Reflecting now on what has changed
Left behind a life of chains

Life reviewed cycle done
Back to having so much fun

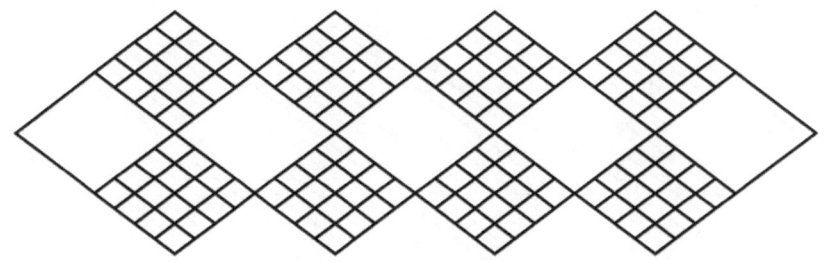

Validation sought for a fix
Playing around with head game tricks

Heavy sorrow weighing heart down
I need some help so I don't drown

Affliction addiction anxiety
Can't escape what I use to be

Interior landscape weed growing soil
Misled ambition as to toil

Glitching in action direction unknown
Insecurity in every bone

Why me why now so intense
Trainwreck carnage from past tense

Hold me guide me show me light
Make in me all things bright

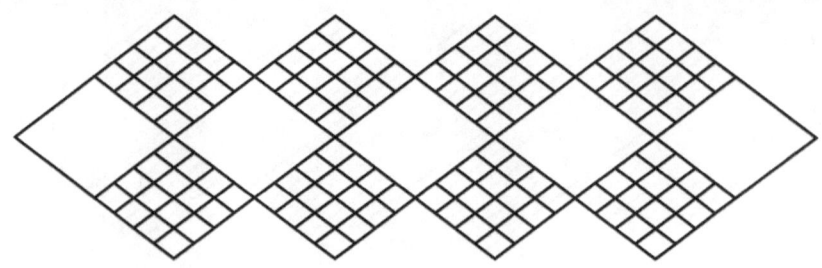

*Chronic victimhood syndrome reveals*
*Prescription writing and kickback deals*

*Treating the symptoms ignoring the core*
*Creating one big revolving door*

*Side effects suicide chemical coma*
*A drug is a drug and no I don't know ya*

*Peeling layers collapsing the coo*
*Calling out sickness brought by the who*

*A virus so lethal no one survives*
*Except for lifted with stars in their eyes*

*Too much to chew value of nill*
*Empty cup broken nothing to spill*

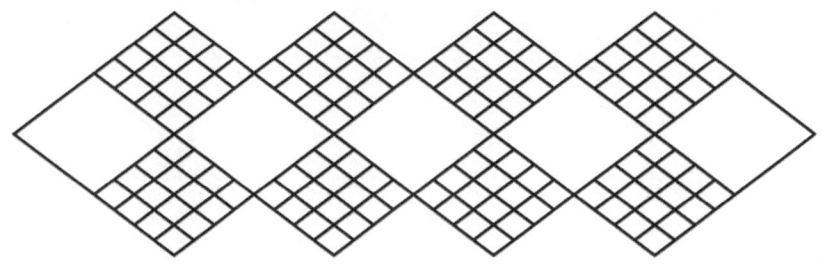

Suffering seems more intense
The longer our lives are lived around dense

Unaware oblivious
Ignorance is true bliss

Blind to laws trapped by thought
Can't get up off the pot

What conformity has for thee
Ask and receive grow your own tree

Gilded inner cut in half
Not enough time for a laugh

Sick and sad climbing rungs
Criticism from most tongues

Gut check baby get strapped up
Carry yourself with a full cup

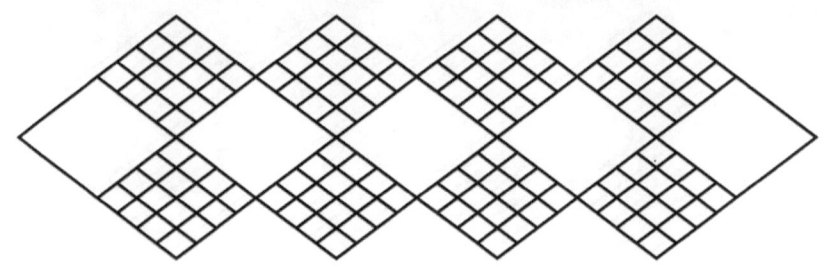

Growing what has been given
In a way that promotes sound liven

Background checks gut instincts
Knowing what and where are stinks

Past agendas into each soul
As we see as we know

Independent from powers reign
Propagandas wolves need slain

Poster child entrenched by sly
As stolen talent passes by

Coat tail poison seeping through
Laying claim to me and you

Used and discarded in the name
Revolving door of hurt and pain

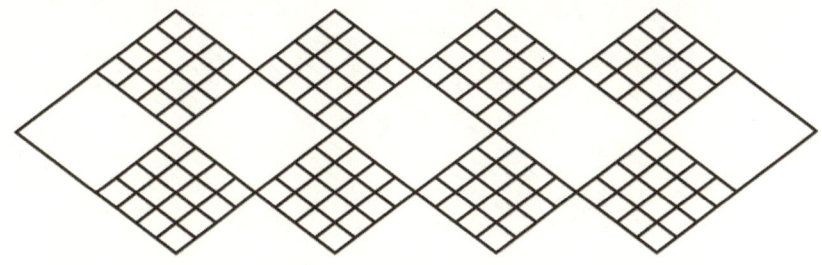

List of labors torched and scorched
Pulling strings from some porch

Strange endeavors telling tales
Put together without nails

Heart of envy jealous gains
As the sickle slices grains

Stock to stork bean to baby
On the hope of just maybe

Neverending source to see
Why the kingdoms had to be

Lasting layers truth be told
Amazing what we do hold

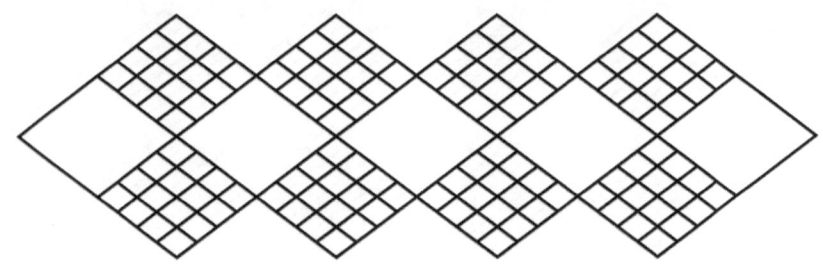

Audacious plethora of circumstance
Subjective boundaries in some dance

Credited crowns desert thornes
Clowns collecting they acorns

Collective conscience forming thoughts
As we get what we got

Congrats collision to express
What and why we have duress

Emotional body cut to shreds
Inflicted with what's been reds

Cataclysmic detour sign
What was once now don't shine

Clear in clarity towers fall
Here to build not drop the ball

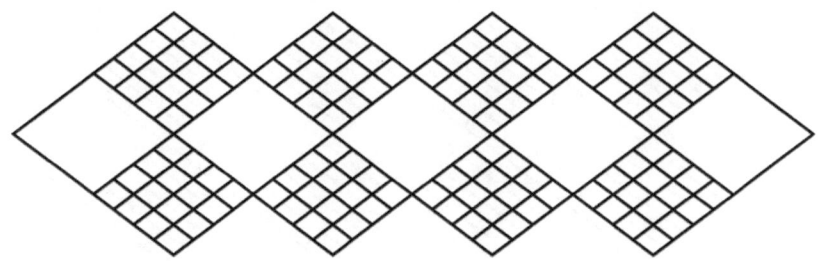

Shaving through doubts that arise
Keeping my word all despise

Feeling so empty facing betrayal
What was once now a fail

Tired of reaching too tired to try
Setting that dream free to fly

Holding hope give to get
Can't accept a life of shit

Circular motion swept away
Manifesting a brand new day

Glad to see through smoke and mirrors
As I rise to above my peers

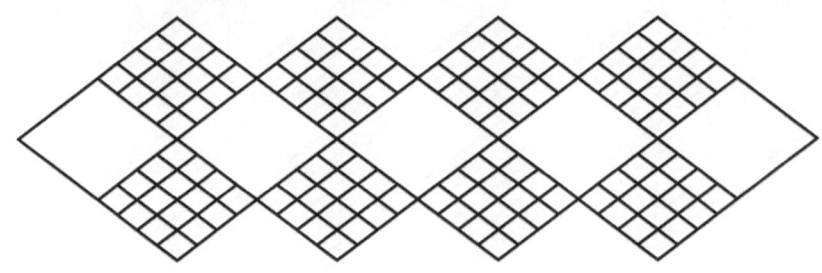

*If you get lost in a sea of souls*
*I'll be here holding our rose*

*Putting you back on our shared path*
*Forever entangled not alone in our craft*

*Impression impacting triggering growth*
*Loyalty looming protecting our oath*

*Forward in motion leading the way*
*Being the sun that shines everyday*

*Next to inherit what is deserved*
*What we put in how we must serve*

*You got this kind soul look for what's good*
*Step into your role that has withstood*

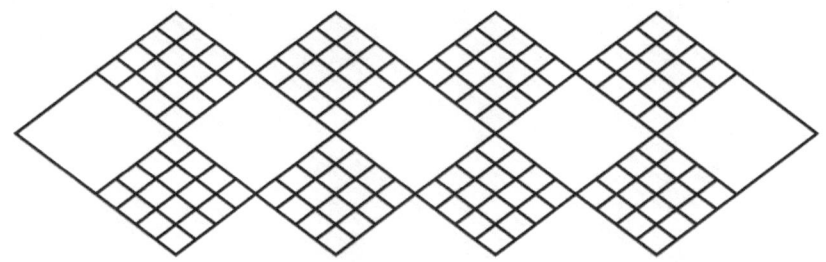

Overwhelmed by what life offers
Gotta detach from the scoffers

Negative nellies push and pull
Going against my own will

Feeling a target square on my back
Please help me out of this life so wack

Hearing my calling path of my own
In my dreams I was shown

Quieting external listening deep
No attention paid to the wolf or the sheep

Memories fleeting out with the hurt
Around the perimeter is where I skirt

It's my life leave me alone
Your opinion has a negative tone

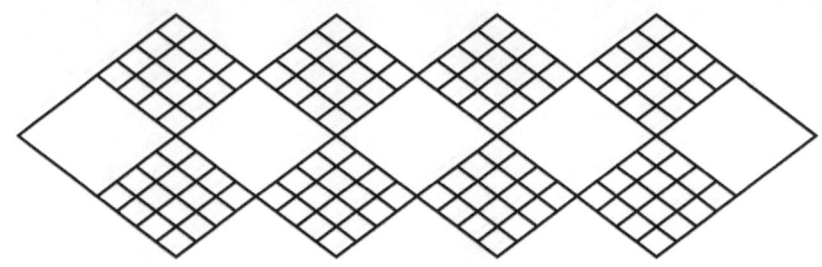

Black eyed beauty it's your turn
For the heartache and its burn

Tearing at me fangs and claws
Manipulating your own sick cause

Stripping me of joy and hope
It was easier to get off dope

Had my attention held my heart
Now it lays bleeding ripped apart

I didn't betray you so don't blame me
Take your scorned heart and let me be

Thanks for the lesson now stay away
My tab is paid with heart I pay

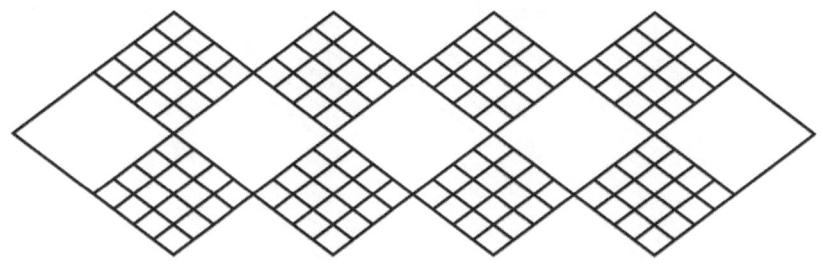

Writing rhymes to keep me sane
As I slay what is a drain

People places this and that
With what's imbued under each hat

Revised records sent and said
He who wins he who bled

Detrimental cover up
Always just never corrupt

Trusting instinct powering through
A mess created by the stew

Mix and mingle authoritate
Changing time lines before it's too late

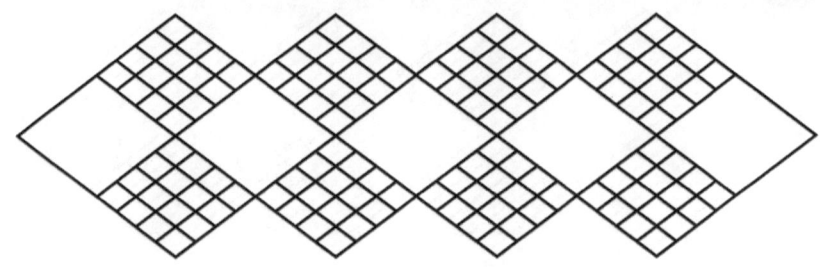

Contemptuous denial of others will
Conversation permeates of as still

Contemplation gaslite trip
Guzzling wine not a sip

Classic control wrapped in faith
Expanding out from a base

Sticky ointment screwed and blued
Without wisdom in tattoo

Introspection not deflection
Cliff ahead at intersection

Cotton candy lollipops
Over reach authority not always the cops

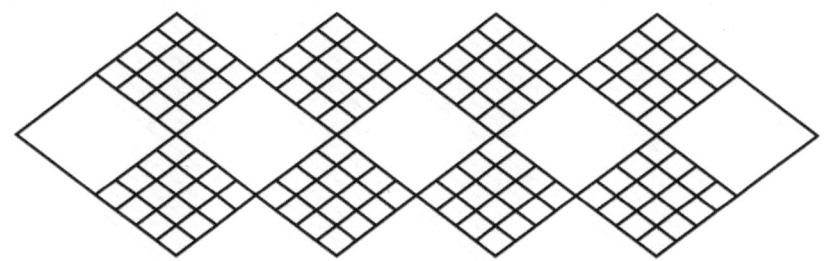

Looking over seeing through
Not the one or the who

Humble pride confidence
Calling in a true romance

Collecting credit behind the scenes
In each lifetime so it seems

Enjoying rest spent alone
Missing the stars and my home

Here again one more term
Once forgotten now must learn

Sage like presence still water deep
What is sewn shall we reap

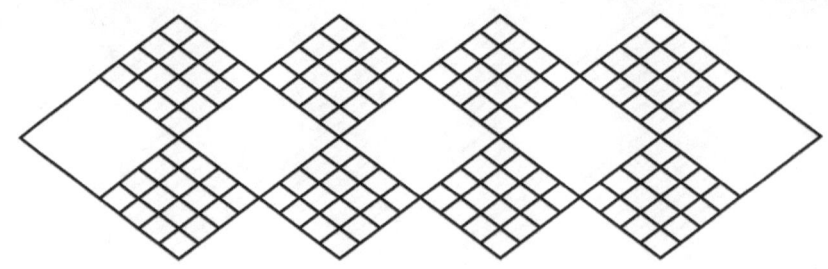

What I give what you take
Without balance for goodness sake

Drained emotions energy hung
Out on a limb connection done

Enabled and rescued looking backs
The weight of heartache it do packs

The hurt keep brimming as memories fade
In the sunlight where we once played

Never a thought to destroy
I loved you like a brand new toy

Now I travel away through the fog
Looking for water like a panting dog

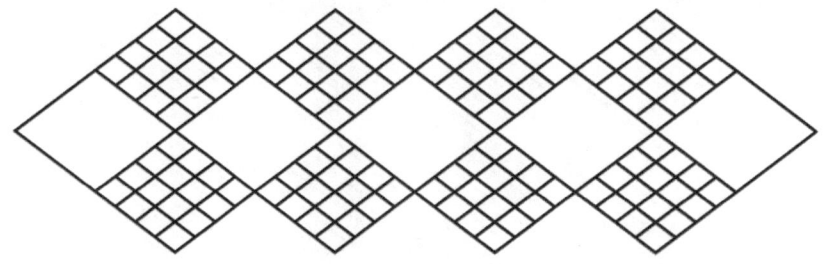

Through the wind serendipitous songs
Hold the thoughts of rights and wrongs

Kismet calling Mariah's mind
All in one for our kind

Programmed procedures DNA strands
Dotted about on mother's lands

Apparatus arranged procedure procured
We dont give a damn about man made fears

Habitual contraption rigged for the fall
Policy programmed by the kabal

Method of madness mode not a fluke
Violent behavior making me puke

Circumstantial niche power prevails
For our coffins with its nails

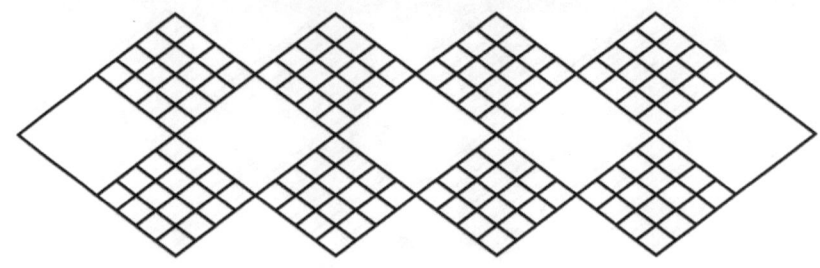

Taken advantage of precious grace
Welling of guilt writ on the face

Action required decision made
Not that important to get laid

Appreciation hack nowhere to run
Nowhere to hide having no more fun

Fall on your own sword mine's in its sheath
Maybe someday you'll find relief

Obligation to burden falsehoods surreal
Disgusting dogma you know the spiel

Realistic pain energy filled
Think about all the blood it's spilled

Dark cloud dungeon low in vibe
Glad I'm on the other side

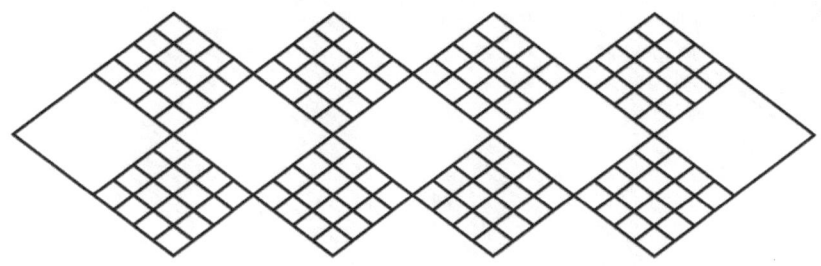

Heart space closed for a while
Till I heal from that smile

Thought it was meant to be
Our future love endlessly

No blame to place just didn't workout
The end was cordial no one had to shout

With heart in the lead I'll travel on
To find the sun to find the one

I know she's here I know her name
I know her love will drive me insane

Dedicated to reunite so our love can ignite

A spark so bright a brilliant glow
A kind of love with all the flow

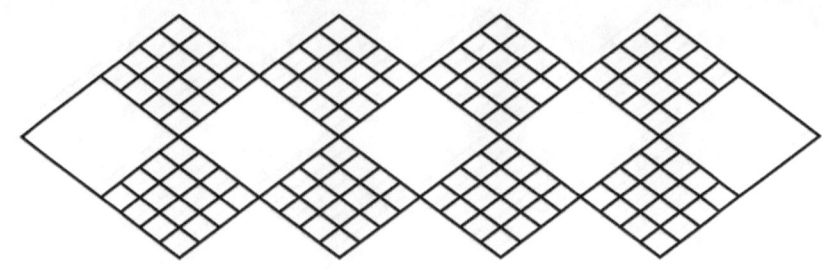

When love hurts what's this mean
In this world in between

Tears of loss another heartache
Gave what I had and seldom take

10 more lessons 10 more years
Better than 20 years of bears

Is love real or just a word
Why do heart matters seem so absurd

Come on now gimme a break
Find me a true love without a stake

Lumarian wisdom dwells within
Doing our best to start over again

Heart space open guided within
On this face is a grin

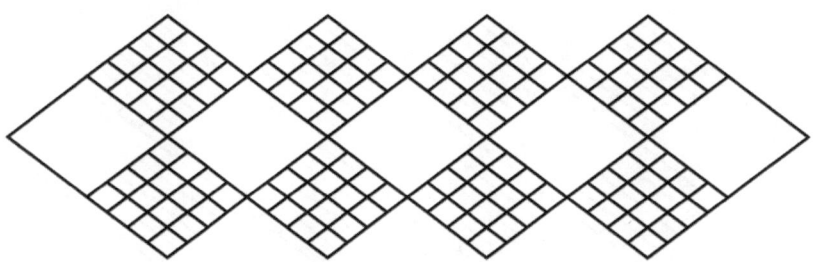

Above the godhead seducing science
Without wisdom without compliance

Slippery slope slithering down
Unneeded path of the rational clown

Projecting its poison up on its perch
Just might be worse than the negative church

Suggesting the means ignoring the cause
No awareness of the universes laws

Negative nodules holding us back
Science is high probably on crack

Cosmic collapse heading aware
So find your purpose and be willing to dare

Take back our heart take back our power
Sadistic in science the fauci hour

Culmination cause and effect
DNA mystery creation I bet

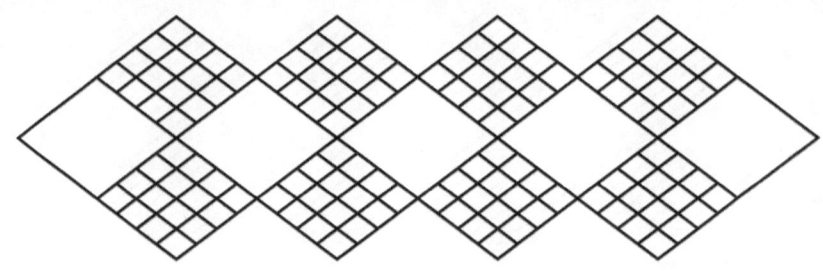

One last time here we go again
Catching the blame for where I've been

Manipulative lip service lies at the core
No appreciation for what we've bore

Disrespect stubborn and hard
Unaware of the inner card

Parasite in nature needing a host
Bragging of stupid always a boast

Innate awareness trauma bond
In the past lives that are gone

Not this time deck is full
Royal flush no jokers fool

Out of my own way surrendered to source
Being honest this of course

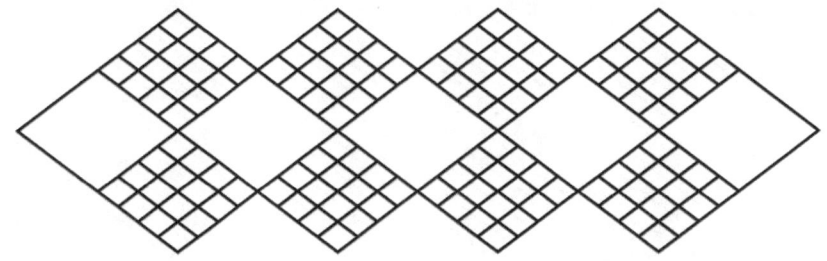

Orchestrate your own fate

Proudly paddle steady and slow
Stop listening to the bull

Constant constraints opinionated
So much law in each state

Bold and break-n goal in sight
Feel the field day and night

So connected hidden strength
Only one source do I thank

Science suckers hold your ball
Newton's laws can't explain it all

Metaphysics where its at
Like the magician and his hat

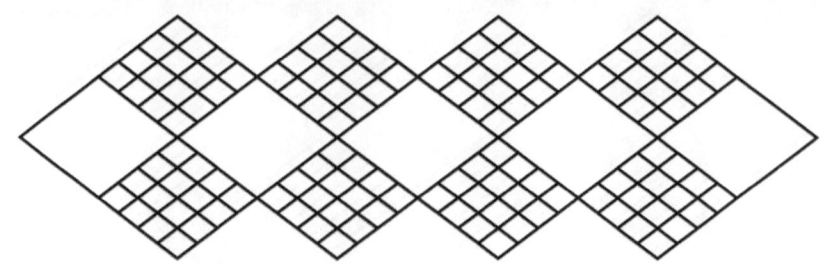

Six day creation seventh day sleep
Blinding the masses fleecing the sheep

Wealth beyond measure measuring sin
Procrastination commanding kin

Doorbell ringing nobody home
White froth on the mouth I am shone

Melancholy mattress asleep at the wheel
No one safe from what they steal

Another head taken another lie faken
Fat of the pig isn't that bacon

Fleas of a dog thief in the night
Invoking power down for a fight

Condescending carnival of the mad
Collecting the dollars that you had

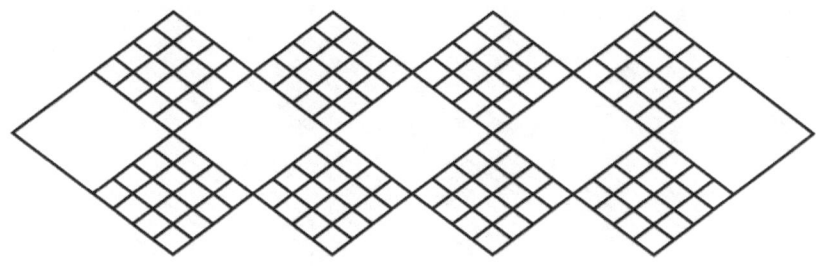

Not gonna beg for a date
But this heart is feeling fate

High vibration has lead me here
In these eyes I see clear

This heart needs the love you have
You are not my other half

I'll stay patient ill stay idle
Until we claim our true title

Nothing nowhere can prevent
Anything that was meant

My love for you is all that's real
On this path that's made for two

Souls entangled for so long
Please don't fear our lovely song

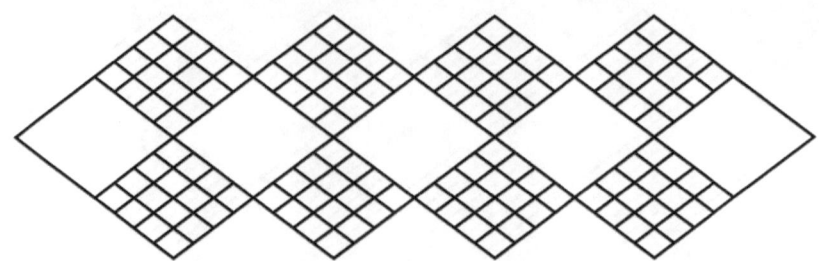

*Obligation and pressure try to pretend*
*They are the way that they are a friend*

*Burnout bottle neck seeking to achieve*
*Can't take with what we must leave*

*Fingers worked down to the bone*
*Broken back without a home*

*American dream in this realm*
*Wack job lunatics at the helm*

*Pumping the slave race for all its worth*
*Never enough in its purse*

*Corporation the worst kind*
*Obey your master laws define*

*Privileged rights for the rich*
*Making my life sort of a bitch*

*Not gonna take it this time around*
*Gonna burn power the the ground*

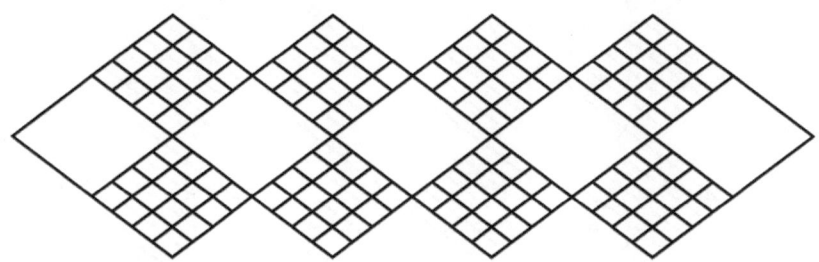

Boredom breeding pyramid schemes
These realities not what it seems

Traditions tied brave men died
Surfers ride churches lied

Emotionally abused spiritual death
Hopeless discontent with each breath

Perpetrator of borrowed laws
Conquering kingdoms control the cause

Hitlers 3 reich roman rule
Using death as its tool

Billions spent billion died
Still enslaved while the mother cried

Drunk on power cant give up
Taking a piss in our cup

Wipe the slate even the field
Let your heart produce the yield

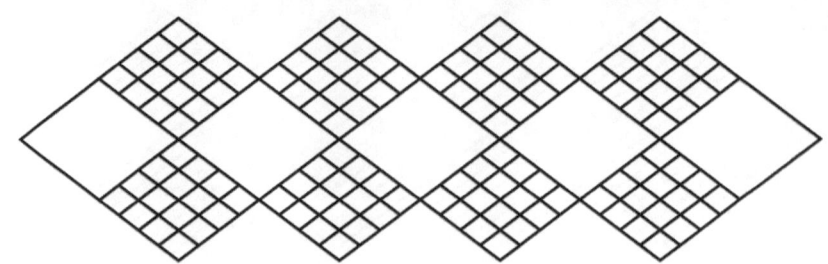

*Out of reach for so long*
*In that love of my song*

*Vibration that fills my soul*
*One with source that makes me whole*

*Cannot take what can't be seen*
*Perfect cover from the machine*

*Corporate grinder greedy desire*
*On our blood it gets higher*

*Save a buck cutting loose*
*Heads of slaves in its noose*

*Like it cares loyalty lost*
*Give one finger to the boss*

*Trying to break us won't give up*
*Even after it steals your cup*

*Fearful fossils dinosaurs*
*We the sluts they the whores*

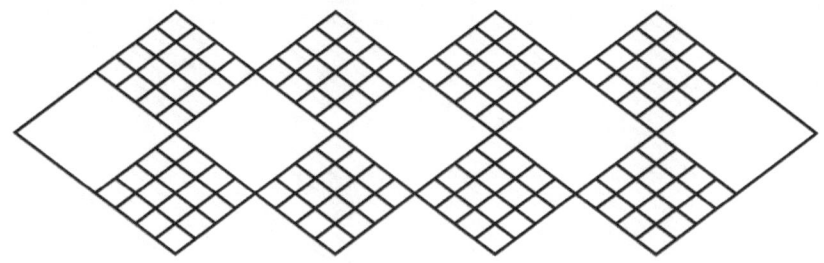

In the still a voice is heard
Helping me write every word

Gifted heart bleeding hands
Hard fought journey that demands

Ever present wondering
Living life like it's a dream

Grounded solid to the earth
Mystic magic giving birth

Wisdom beaming forgotten tales
Guided always like the whales

New beginning once again
All the while atoning sin

Ditching dead wood planting seeds
What's the purpose of the needs

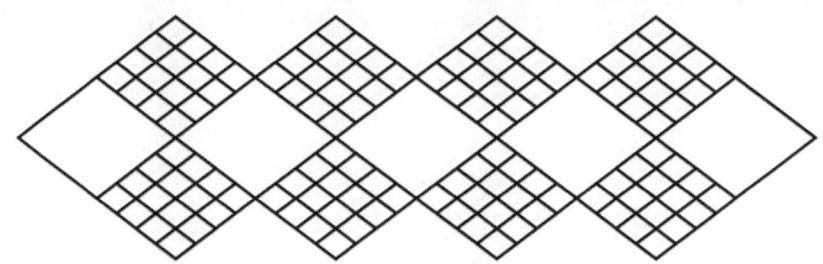

Classic collapse classic rebirth
Energy growing on mother earth

Cosmic alignment cannot be stopped
Then will see who's on top

Watch the glimmer wield each truth
In the hour we get proof

Oz Alice Dorothy's dream
Missing only is one last scene

Crazy twist insane design
All to teach us how to shine

Saddle up change is here
No more tv or drinking beer

Material madness of the rich
Pain in the ass like to bitch

Low vibration backstab fools
Already dead without tools

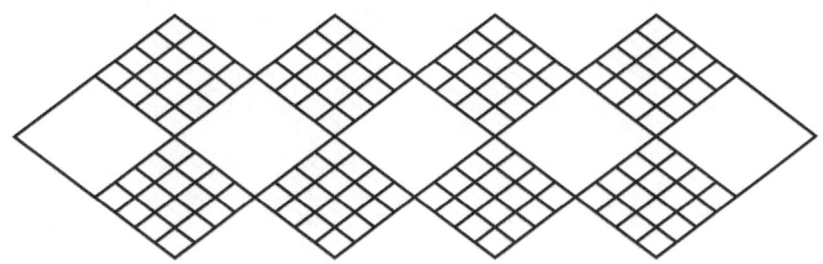

Broken heart wounded soul
Each and every has a role

Lessons learnt bridges burnt
On a high way of the dirt

One way forward no stop signs
Calm and collective by design

Peering into this and that
Trap is set for the rat

Incubation thoughts reveal
On just what it takes to heal

Wisdom flowing it comes with ease
Don't need help no thank you please

Dark dilemmas stay away
You cannot wreck my day

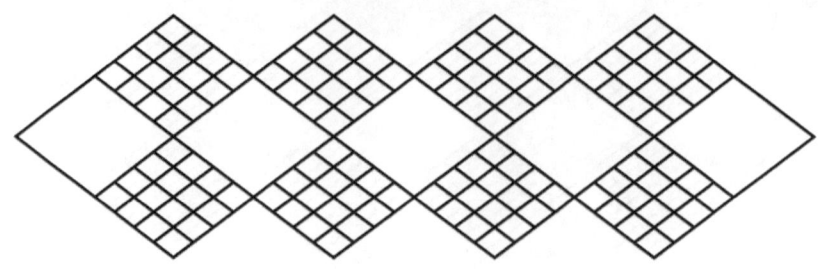

*Befuddled amazement confused perplexed*
*So much stuff out of context*

*Flabbergast dumb found bewilderment*
*Flustered dizzy discontent*

*Baffled dazed fickleness*
*Are the signs of distress*

*Arbitrary to what defines*
*It's a choice to release what confines*

*Frivolous erratic inconsistent ways*
*Petty impractical foolish days*

*Absurd irrational illogical deeds*
*Shameless cowards of bad seeds*

*Foe of the flower friend to greed*
*Just like ivy greed is a weed*

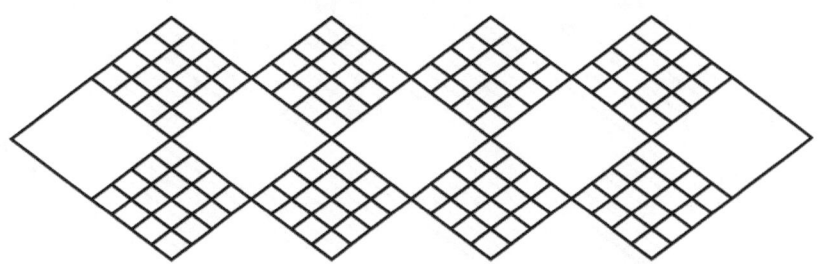

What was ever meant to be
Here and now for the free

Brave enough to break the bonds
Negative ties that be holding on

Ridiculed out of envy's view
Jealousy so many spue

Waste not want not however that goes
Disposable society has its woes

Elected officials deeply entrenched
Bought and paid for no common sense

Follow the money and behold
Spineless cowards on the road

To a roman empire of sorts
The kind that allows you one pair of shorts

Freedom fought for freedom within
No false flag will happen again

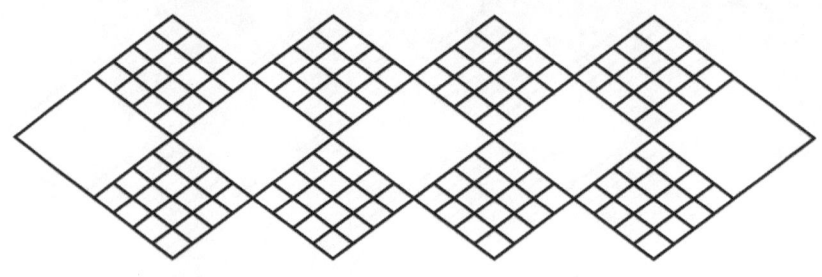

*Soaring ever higher not giving to desire*

*Passing each test no longer a guest*

*Being who I am before my life began*

*Tic- tac- toe one move left to go*

*Alchemizing rhyme messages sublime*

*Confetti I'm so ready not another plate of spaghetti*

*Nearly lost my mind becoming so divine*

*Kind and giving makes life worth living*

*Give and get feeling lit*

*Poised and calm for the human bomb*

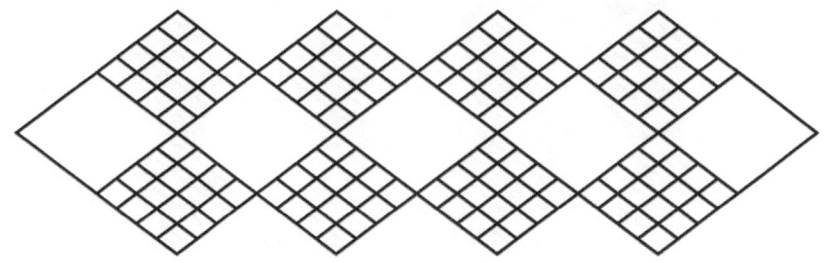

Hitmen hired to fight its wars
With the gold that it stores

Organized chaos of the lost
Its tradition will have a cost

Chosen to lead not to rule
Big mistake of this fool

Can't give up its greedy way
Of the fire it does play

Taking the high road escaping attack
On a horse with a broken back

Chrome polished shimmer turned to rust
Salt of the earth under her crust

Bring your bots show your face
From under a rock is your place

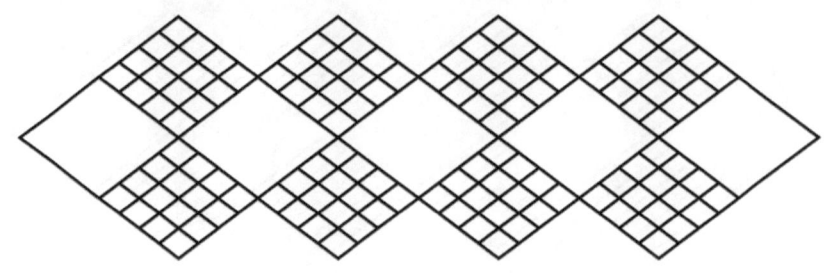

*Split in half for a while*
*Back together with a smile*

*So much groth carried on*
*These broad shoulders that are braun*

*Here to laugh here to play*
*Breaking free from the old way*

*Don't understand of course its change*
*Transforming pain out on this plain*

*Echoing whispers full steam ahead*
*Don't have time for the dead*

*Pick a vibration feel its hold*
*Then to the next confident and bold*

*Contrasting colors vivid define*
*From where we come and how we shine*

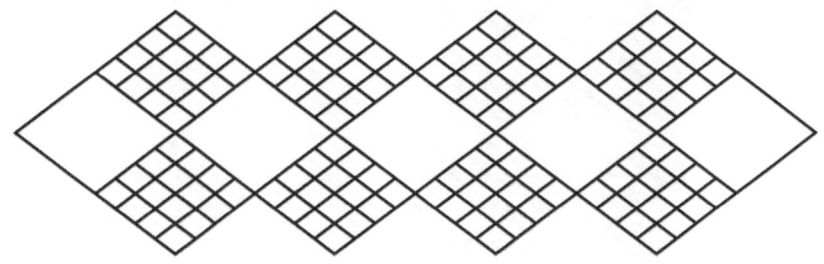

Rapture rodents religious bile
Causing fear with a smile

Sensing sickness from that perch
Inequality of the church

This branch that branch correlate
Projecting future human fate

Here's one for you of the light
Put down the front and get right

Collapsing empire outside in
Sickened shepherds greedy grin

Luxury life using lord
Get your scissors cut the cord

Condescending proclamation
Has a way to corrupt a nation

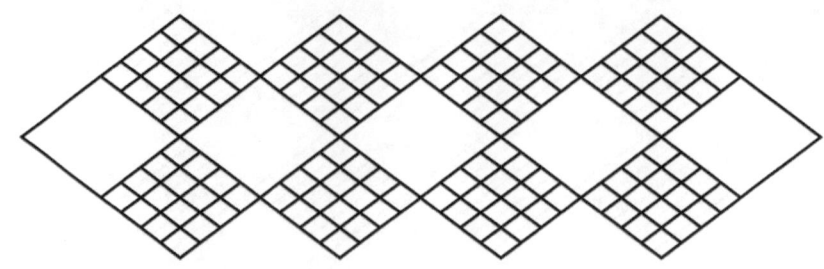

More or less just a friend
But here's my love I can't pretend

Enigmatic mystics way
To bring love and save the day

No conditions open seam
Stand with me and live this dream

Accumulate brave and strong
Everything good nothing wrong

Heart that matters opinions not
Coming together is always hot

Immersed in passion lovers card
My gift for you is very hard

Really sweetie it's our time
Show me your heart here is mine

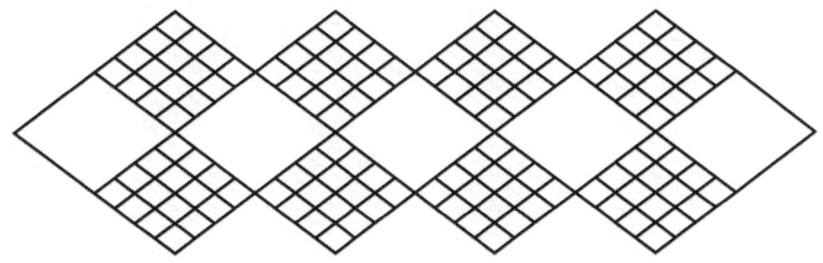

Fools of conformity breaking in
Attempting to steal what was given

Botched attempt robbery exposed
No more life out in the cold

Deep engrainment traditional ties
In the darkness hiding its eyes

Prophets purged climbing higher
My own truth my desire

All illusion fabricate
Of the nasty headless snake

Jack and jill Adam and Eve
All made up make believe

Setting the tone coming hard
No longer the victim of the tard

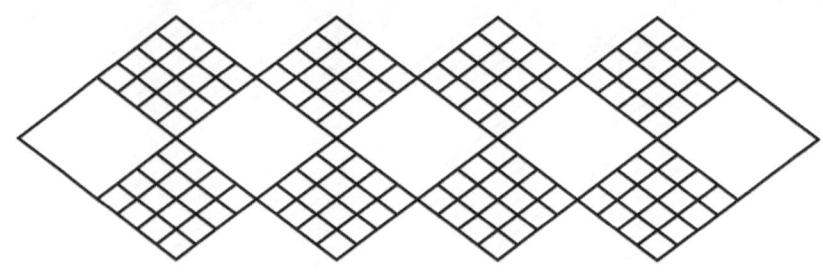

Seed of fear where is it from
One guess and that's dumb

Articles addressing perpetuation
All the while causing stagnation

Tax free dollars in the name
Ready and willing to place blame

Hidden intentions glorified
In control to pacify

Our inner truth honest and bold
Threat to the man authority sold

Bad bill of goods bent on desire
Threatening some lake of fire

Stand back and watch what true loves about
Reconsider control and trust without doubt

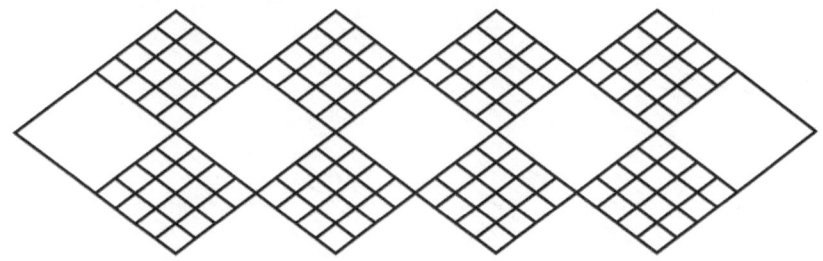

Freedoms handshake releasing guilt
And the shame religion built

Not its captive not its slave
Immune to the poison that it gave

Hermit rising phoenix sun
Purification will be done

Axis tilting to pure love
Are your ready here's your shove

Ferris wheel of circus clowns
Trespass on these sacred grounds

Not a warning just beware
Change is here so do prepare

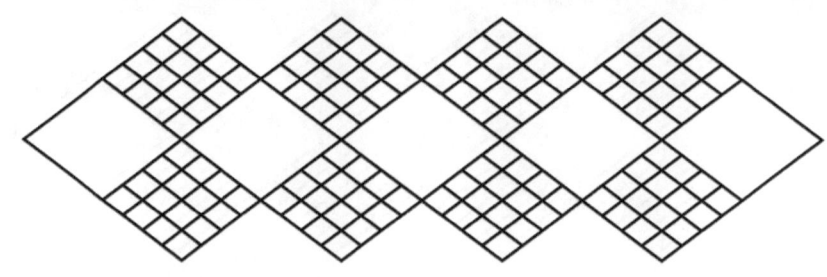

Work as a slave die in a grave

Emotional whip power the trip

Cascading crown pointing down

Elaborate ruse secular muse

Allegorically wrong cannot belong

Confusion caused breaking laws

Hopelessly lost free will the cost

Polarized within chickens begin

Clucking without voices in doubt

Delirious dimension as to mention

Higher self goal selfless with soul

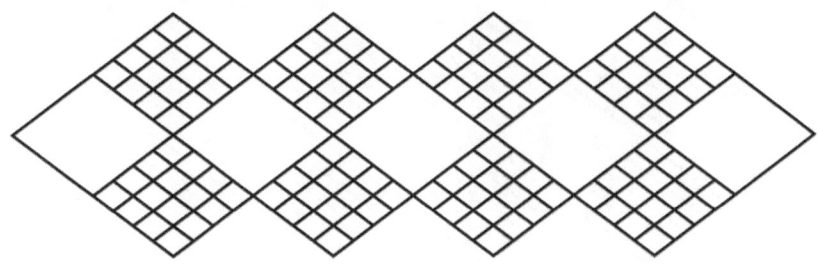

Cut from a cloth torn from a tree
Here to be bold wild and free

Paradigm shift good for the soul
Out of what was made by a troll

Leaders lead power controls
Look around who are the trolls

Stale chips open bag
On a perch mouth to nag

Hold on lets back up
You wanna put what in my cup

Prestigious authority collusion and crimes
Greedy filth of the slimes

Lol watch your six
From the sky will come your bricks

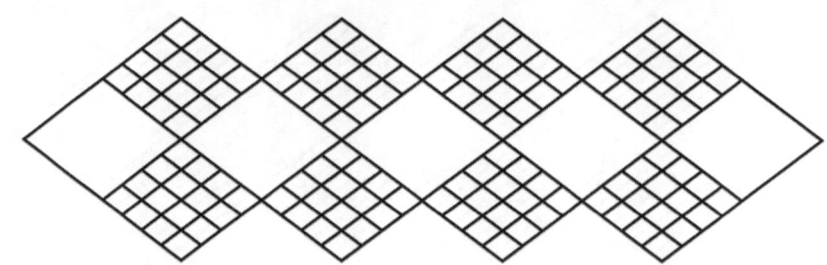

Naked and lost what's gone down
Where is my home in what town

Insanity rules corporate ghouls
Confounding conformity of the fools

Sell outs selling sick and sad
Trapped in what is a glad and mad

Express delivery chocolate cake
Emotions eaten hard to flake

Arduous journey back to source
Sails set a natural course

Into the wind eye of the storm
With the strength to subdue the swarm

Glory goons pious pricks
Not sure there can be a fix

Steady steering another day
Free to laugh have fun and play

## To Powers Intentions

Salvation seekers archetype
The real purpose of this hype

Built on lies on top of tales
White mens fire red hot nails

Ignorance destroys wisdom preserves
Path of destruction gets what it deserves

Fire starting fairies here's your match
Rotten eggs do not hatch

Generations built on cruel
Energy wasted by the fool

Dotted atrocities holy wars
To control all its whores

Vortex dragging down the vibe
Win at all cost of the hive

Can't decide what is worse
God or humans and this curse

www.ingramcontent.com/pod-product-compliance
Lightning Source LLC
LaVergne TN
LVHW041536070526
838199LV00046B/1690